MARKETING SECRETS OF THE ULTRA-WEALTHY

COOPER SAUNDERS

© Copyright 2023 - All rights reserved.

The content contained within this book may not be reproduced, duplicated or transmitted without direct written permission from the author or the publisher.

Under no circumstances will any blame or legal responsibility be held against the publisher, or author, for any damages, reparation, or monetary loss due to the information contained within this book, either directly or indirectly.

Legal Notice:

This book is copyright protected. It is only for personal use. You cannot amend, distribute, sell, use, quote or paraphrase any part, or the content within this book, without the consent of the author or publisher.

Disclaimer Notice:

The publisher and the author make no representations or warranties with the respect to the accuracy or completeness of the contents of this work and specifically disclaim all warranties, including without limitation warranties of fitness for a particular purpose. No warranty may be created or extended by sales or promotional materials. The methods and strategies contained in this book may not be suitable for every situation. This work is sold with the understanding that the publisher is not engaged in rendering legal, accounting or other professional services. The author shall not be liable for damages arising therefrom. The reader should be aware that methods of marketing are always changing and should always double check methods and websites before implementing.

For general information email

Info@wiseguysdigitalmarketing.com

CONTENTS

Part 1: THE SECRET FORMULA	1
Chapter One: Begin With The End In Mind	5
Chapter Two: Identify The Target Market	19
Chapter Three: Influencing Target Market	31
Chapter Four: Understanding The Basics Of Digital Marketing	43
PART 2: IMPLEMENT THE TACTICS!	71
Chapter Five: Your Bait	73
Chapter Six: Creating The Advertisements	93
Chapter Seven: Capture The Lead	113
Chapter Eight: Conversions	125
Chapter Nine: Building From The Ground Up	147
PART 3: WRAPPING IT UP	161
Chapter Ten Market Research	163
Chapter Eleven: Breaking Down Psychology	173
Conclusion	197
About the Author	235

This book is dedicated to my loving parents, my two sweet beagles, and the love of my life, Bailey.
Without you guys, this would not have been possible.
Thank you.

PART 1
THE SECRET FORMULA

The secret formula will show you how to obtain consistent and predictable results from your marketing efforts. Most business owners market their company a lot like gambling, throwing their money around without knowing what works and what doesn't. On the other hand, the UltraWealthy have a method that works more like a vending machine rather than a slot machine. For example, what happens when you use a vending machine? You walk up, put in your dollar, and key in the code for your desired snack. You simply get what you paid for!

Unfortunately, most companies don't have this experience when trying to grow their business. For them, it is more like visiting a slot machine. They enter their money, pull the lever, and pray that they get something out of it. There is no method, and it is all based on luck. Most of the time, the odds are stacked against them. Why? Because they are not taking the time to set up a proper strategy that will generate results! They may get lucky here and there, but nothing substantial—just enough for them to keep going until they run out of marketing dollars.

For my 21st birthday, my family took me to Las Vegas, one week before my actual birthday. While all of my family was out on the casino floor, I got to watch and observe from a distance.

I believe that God works in mysterious ways because while I was watching all of these people

lose all of their hard-earned money, it hit me. These people who are just pulling a lever at the slot machine, hoping to make some return on their investment, are no different from most business owners when marketing their companies!

Sometimes business owners even admit that they have no idea what works and what doesn't when marketing their company. They are just throwing dollars out there, hoping to hit the jackpot.

> *"Half the money I spend on advertising is wasted; the trouble is I don't know which half."*
> **- John Wanamaker, Famous American Merchant.**

What?! This form of marketing is the standard, but it does not have to be this way. To make matters worse, some marketing companies also play into this hype for their clients with flashy charts and innovative new ideas. They pump their client's brain full of dopamine, just like the casinos do. At the end of the day, can you rely on achieving the results you want every time? You cannot rely on this strategy to grow your business. Don't get me wrong. You will make mistakes when marketing your company. You will have marketing campaigns that flop. I know this first hand. If you had two options, which would you choose?

Option A: With this option, you are almost always guaranteed to lose your money. You are basing all of your results on luck, and you take no time or planning to ensure that you achieve the best outcome.

Or,

Option B: This option, you are almost always guaranteed to get a return on your investment. You take the time

Part 1: THE SECRET FORMULA

to set up a strategy, and you are basing all of your results on proven plans that have worked in the past.

Option A seems pretty ridiculous, but that is how 90% of business owners advertise their company. We are going to change that.

This section will help you create a solid foundation for your digital marketing campaign so that it doesn't feel like going to the casino when you are marketing your company! We will hit on the first steps you will need to take to create your vending machine marketing plan. Building a solid foundation is one of the most critical parts of the process.

Making sure you take the time to establish a rock-solid foundation when marketing your

company is crucial. Imagine you want to create the tallest building in your city. You find the construction company and discuss your vision and goals, and you decide to hire them. After three years, the building is completed! You have invested massive amounts of time and money, so you are ready to see the finished product.

You hop in the car with your family, and you are so excited for them to see the result of all of the work you have put in these past years. When you arrive, something looks off. It is slightly tilted. Upon further inspection, you realize you never took the time to set up the proper foundation. You built your building on a sandy foundation!! The whole project is scrapped, and all you can do is lick your wounds and start from square one.

Seeing that the foundation was the real problem is the best-case scenario. Most of the time, business owners do not realize that it wasn't the building but the foundation that made the whole campaign a waste. They go and hire another marketing company, and their terrible experience happens again and again until they can no longer take it. They either go out of business or focus on referral business.

Remember, take the time to make sure your foundation is solid, and take the necessary steps in this section to start visiting the vending machine instead of the casino! If you are in charge

of marketing for your company and are thinking about hiring a digital marketing company and they don't touch on this, run for the hills.

CHAPTER ONE: BEGIN WITH THE END IN MIND

"Let others get caught up in the twist and turns of the everyday battle, relishing their little victories. Grand Strategy will bring you the ultimate reward: the last laugh."
-**Robert Greene, 48 Laws Of Power**

What qualities do some of the most successful humans and companies have that all others don't? You see, success leaves clues, and it is our job as humans to pick up on these clues and act upon them, evolve. If we didn't evolve, we would still be in caves, living off the land, competing with the rest of the animal kingdom. Is it by chance or luck that since the dawn of time, every single successful group or entity has followed the same pattern—no matter how large or small? No.

From Alexander the Great down to the modern-day corporation, they all have one thing in common. They understood their Grand Strategy and had the grit to complete what they set their minds to, the one end goal they are striving to achieve. So the question is, why do some people ignore these clues? Wouldn't it be easier if they just follow what works, or is it merely that that just have no idea? Are they truly that oblivious, or is it something else?

To gather some context, we need to step back and understand how humans separated from the rest of the animal kingdom in the first place. In Robert Greene's book, The 33 Strategies of War, he says, "Thousands of years ago, we humans elevated ourselves above the animal world and never looked back. Figuratively speaking, the key to this evolutionary advance was our powers of vision: language and the ability to reason that it gave us, let us see more of the world around us. To protect itself from a predator, an animal depending on its senses and instincts; it could not see around the corner, or to the other end of the forest.

"We humans, on the other hand, could map the entire forest, study the habits of dangerous animals and even nature itself, gaining deeper, wider knowledge of our environment. We could see the dangers coming before they were here. This expanded vision was abstract: where an animal is locked in the present, we could see into the past and glimpse as far as our reason would take us into the future. Our insight expanded further and further into time and space, and we came to dominate the world."

This is the key that I want you to see. Very few people nowadays utilize this fantastic tool that got us here in the first place—drifting wherever the wind takes them, no direction at all.

Chapter One: Begin With The End In Mind

"In a world where people are increasingly incapable of thinking consequently, more animal than ever, the practice of grand strategy will instantly elevate you above others."
-Robert Greene

Our strength is not that we are the fastest or the strongest in the animal kingdom. Our power is that we are able to see what we want, create a plan on how to get there, and get it done. Building on past mistakes and learning from them.

This is nothing new. This is how humans survived and evolved. We were able to have vision, and we were able to plan tactics and strategies to get us out of harmful situations before they happened. This is how we were able to control the animal kingdom completely. This is why we dominate the sky, land, and ocean.

Even with this extraordinary strength that God blessed humanity with, we find ourselves in bad situations. Society got too comfortable. Life is now too easy compared to our primal days. We no longer have to worry about a saber tooth tiger entering our cave in the middle of the night.

How was Alexander The Great able to conquer the entire Persian Empire before the age that most of us are allowed to have a beer? From birth, his mother gave him a clear destiny and goal: to rule the known world. From the age of three, he could see in his mind's eye the role he would play when he was thirty. He was trained to master his emotions, and understood the tactical moves he must make. He always was thinking ahead, saying to himself,

"This action will advance me toward my goal; this one will lead me nowhere."

He had a Grand Strategy, and once he had that, he developed tactical objectives to get there, and then everything else fell into place. He also had excellent teachers that helped him along the way.

When you are trying to grow your company, there is a system in place, a solid plan that has already worked for centuries. All you have to do is follow it. Starbucks has a Grand Strategy, "To inspire and nurture the human spirit – one person, one cup, and one neighborhood at a time." Every move Starbucks makes, they can look back and ask themselves, "Will this action move us toward our goal, or away from it?"

That's it. That is the exact method that every single successful person or organization took to achieve victory. They established a clear Grand Strategy and then took steps to achieve the goals, but seeing where you want to end up is the easy part.

So why do some people ignore these clues? Wouldn't it be easier if they just follow what works? Are they indeed that oblivious, or is it something else? As the saying goes, "If it were more information we needed, we would all be rich and have six-packs." The information is here, and it's always been here.

I believe that what separates the great companies, people, and organizations is having the grit to see it all the way through. They make the right moves consistently. When you make a long-term plan, you must have a lot of patience and resilience to see it through. At a certain point, you know that eating your body weight in cake is not a good idea, but that is your future self's problem, not yours.

Humans are in love with instant gratification. They want happiness now, even though it will prove to be detrimental down the road. Truly great leaders are able to understand that nothing comes easy, and if it did, everyone would do it.

I can tell within five minutes if a potential client has the grit to implement this strategy. Are they looking for a get rich quick scheme, or are they looking to dominate their industry? There is nothing wrong with wanting a get rich quick scheme, but this is not where you will find it.

Before you start this journey, ask yourself, "Am I in for the long haul, or not?" If you are, get ready for the ride of your life. You might be asking yourself, "Can I really use this method to grow my company?"

My answer is this:

- Humans have used the Grand Strategy to...
- Dominate the Animal Kingdom
- Harness Electricity
- Communicate via Radio Frequencies
- Visit the Moon
- Discover Break Through Medical Treatments
  And much, much more. Yes, I know it will work to grow your company. I'll also walk you through the exact way to build your foundation and guide you through every tactical step you must take to achieve your

Grand Strategy. I'm going to give you the magic formula. Bold claim? You bet.

I can show you how to establish your foundation and employ tactics to get to your desired end goal, but at the end of the day, it's up to you to take action. It's as simple as that.

There are three main aspects of creating a Grand Strategy.

1. Identify Grand Strategy
2. Establish Foundation
3. Establish Tactical Rocks

First Step: Identify Grand Strategy

- $15,000,000 in revenue in 5 years?
- #1 Supplier in the Country by 2026?
- Bring your product to every household in America?
- Every household in the world?

The first step is to choose where you want to go. What is your overall mission for your company? What is the end goal? When you are lying on your death bed, what would have to happen for you to be completely satisfied? Let's assume that there is such a thing.

I want your Grand Strategy to be so massive that it scares you a little bit when you say it. When you can see it in your mind and honestly believe that it is possible, that is when your life will never be the same!

The Man Who Thinks He Can
Poem by Walter D. Wintle

If you think you are beaten, you are
If you think you dare not, you don't,
If you like to win, but you think you can't
It is almost certain you won't.
If you think you'll lose, you're lost
For out of the world we find,
Success begins with a fellow's will
It's all in the state of mind.
If you think you are outclassed, you are
You've got to think high to rise,
You've got to be sure of yourself before
You can ever win a prize.
Life's battles don't always go
To the stronger or faster man,
But soon or late the man who wins
Is the man who thinks he can.

Choose your Grand Strategy, then commit to it. Commit 100% to everything in life, no matter what. The grass is not greener on the other side, trust me.

Second Step: Foundation

The second step we are going to take is to set up a proper foundation. Think about it in this context. Imagine that your Grand Strategy is on the other side of a rushing river. Swimming is not an option. We will build a foundation so that the slippery rocks that we step on won't slide out from underneath us. The rocks you're stepping on to get across the river are your tactical rocks. If you do a superficial job or don't build a foundation at all, you will eventually slip, fall in the river, and die. Rather than you actually dying, it is your dreams, goals, and desires. Personally, I'd rather die than give up on my dreams, goals, and desires. How about you?

Third Step: Tactical Rocks

Now that we understand where we want to go and have the foundation in place, we will develop the steps to get there—one step at a time, with purpose and determination. I'm going to walk you through the exact steps I take with my clients to achieve their desired Grand Strategy for business growth.

Remember, most companies these days are only focusing on the tactical side of things, acting more and more like animals. They are either too lazy or are simply unaware of linking their Grand Strategy. Without the link, you are dead in the water.

Without understanding your Grand Strategy, you will have no idea where you need to go, and eventually, you will get tired and fall into the river. Without establishing the foundation, you will be running in quicksand and eventually get so tired and frustrated you will lay down and die. When you use tactical marketing, you rely on small wins that bring very little long-term success. When you only rely on small tactical victories without a Grand Strategy, you will get lost and ultimately fail. Companies that "cook the books" so that their earnings calls look good are tactical players. They only think of short-term wins, even though the inevitable is coming.

Examples of tactical marketing are slashing your prices, competing solely on price, and using inaccurate sales methods to convince the client that your product or service does something that it does not. When you lie and cheat to get ahead, it will eventually all come crashing down!

Not all companies that just use tactical marketing are bad! Some companies simply do not know the difference. They were told, "Get the most customers in the door by any means necessary!" If this is you, don't worry. This is the new normal for companies. Humans are now so obsessed with instant gratification that they'd rather chose the easy way out rather than taking the time and really create something beautiful. Truly sad.

When you use tactical marketing skills without a long-term strategy, it is like a person with an addiction doing whatever they can to get their next "hit." The more you do it, the harder it is to get off it, just like being addicted to gambling.

This is what you need to be very aware of. If all you did was lose at the casino, they would have no clientele, so they plan the customer's experience flawlessly. While I was sitting in Las Vegas, I decided to watch one guy. He was very particular about which machine he picked. I overheard him talking to his buddy that he wanted to find one that someone had been at for a while. I thought it kind of made sense. The machine would be closer to handing out a big payday.

After a lady that had been sitting there for a while

got up, he promptly sat down and deposited his crisp $100 bill. After about 15 pulls, he was down $55, and then bang! The machine started making all of these loud noises, and colors were lighting up all around him. As people looked over to his machine to watch this lucky fellow, a grin grew across his face like he was the chosen one. He had the Midas touch, simple as that. I even found myself smiling. I mean the colors and sounds; it was infectious! He was now up to $223, and I thought to myself, that's it? After the show that machine put on, I thought he might have won the whole damn casino!

But I continued to watch him after about thirty pulls; he was at about $177. Still not bad! Up $77 in Vegas! A strange thing started to happen, the wins got smaller, and the losses got bigger until he was at a depressing $3.53. As he hit the "cash-out" button, I asked myself why didn't he stop when he was at $223?

Here is the reason—as a human, your brain produces chemicals for pleasure. Two of those chemicals are dopamine and serotonin (more on serotonin later). Dopamine gets pumped into the brain for short term wins, like eating chocolate, hitting the jackpot at the casino— basically getting a quick victory. Dopamine is the part of the brain connected with addiction and what casinos take advantage of to create a loyal customer base.

When you are growing your company, it might feel good getting a client with false advertising or bringing on a client even though your company isn't truly going to solve their needs. It feels good to bring in five new clients even though you needed fifteen to break even. Remember, you are only hurting yourself even though it feels incredible at the moment.

When you use strategic and tactical marketing simultaneously, you will be able to charge what you want and not only be respected in your field but dominate it. The strategic marketing outlook will take a bit more planning, but it will bring massive results in the long term. Now that you understand your Grand Strategy, the rest of this book will show you how to get there.

While I was writing this book, Elon Musk sent out a tweet of his Grand Strategy of what he wanted to achieve back in 2006. It's simple. He knew where he wanted to go. Now all he had to do is figure out how to get there. He had his foundation and Grand Strategy, and that is genuinely all you need. Luckily for you, I am going to give you the step by step tactical plays as well.

Elon 2006:
the master plan is:

1. Build sports car
2. Use that money to build an affordable car
3. Use *that* money to build an even more affordable car
4. While doing above, also provide zero emission electric power generation options

You Will Need Gas

Before we move onto the next chapter, I want to hit on something that I feel many people struggle with when they achieve success, and that is suppressing their dark side. They tell themselves that wanting a great life is selfish, but it's not. Since you were a kid, you were told false prophecies about money and success, and it's B.S. You're supposed to live an abundant and fruitful life. Do not let small-minded people take that away from you.

In Tim S. Grover's book Relentless, he does a fantastic job explaining it this way, "You know the story of Dr. Jekyll and Mr. Hyde? A respected, upstanding doctor discovers a potion that temporarily turns him into a dark, sinister predator, and for a while, he finds he enjoys being free from fear and morality and emotions, not caring about anyone or anything. For the first time in his life, he does what he feels, not what he's been taught."

Welcome to the dark side. I want you to unmask this fabricated persona that society made you put on. I want you to be free and enjoy everything you want to enjoy. Eat whatever you want to eat, travel wherever you want, be yourself, and listen to your heart.

Do you know the people who made the rules? Most likely losers. These might be people that didn't mean you any harm. They just might not know better themselves. They just listened to their parents and accepted it as reality.

A couple of years ago, I told one of my buddies that I was going to start a business.

His 29-year-old brother that still lived in their parents basement overheard me and said, "Ah, are you sure? There is a lot of things that could go wrong. Most businesses go bankrupt in the first year!"

Chapter One: Begin With The End In Mind

I paused for a minute and asked him, "How do you know? Have you ever done it?"

Of course, he hadn't. He got all defensive and gave me one of those generic "good luck's" as most people do when you tell someone a big goal that they truly deep down wish they could do, but they don't because it scares them. They are too worried about what their friends and family would say.

One of my favorite questions to ask is, "How do you know?" Followed by, "Have you ever done it?"

Staple these questions into your memory every time someone wants to unload a heaping pile of B.S. on your dreams. Want to become a millionaire? Don't take advice from your broke aunt. Want to own real estate? Do not take advice from your loser friends. Want to grow a business? Ah, you get my point.

On this journey, you'll be faced with people that will criticize or be flat-out rude to you about your plans or goals. Here's how to deal with this. Don't get upset.

Keep a calm head and reply with, "I am sorry, but I don't take criticism from people I wouldn't take advice from," and leave it at that.

Why am I saying all of this? Because even the fastest sports cars need gas. You need to have the motivation to see this thing through. You are about to change the world. Not only does your future family need you, but the world also needs you. The world needs hope!

I believe in you, and I trust that you will make this world a better place. Some people don't like seeing someone go after their goals because that just reminds them of the ones they gave up on. Stand in the face of criticism, doubt, hatred, and fear and come out victorious.

"Success Requires No Explanation, Failure Permits No Alibis."
-Napoleon Hill, Author of Think and Grow Rich

Remember, the only difference between the successful human and the unsuccessful human is this: the successful human can see the bigger picture and create a plan to achieve their goals.

CHAPTER TWO: IDENTIFY THE TARGET MARKET

"Understand why you are different and how you help, recognize your target market, and give them something they might not even realize they are missing"
– Chris Murry

Now that we have taken the time to understand and develop the overall Grand Strategy for your business, we have to zoom in and focus on the technical side of getting your business to its desired end goal. The first step in creating a successful marketing plan for your company is to identify your target market.

Is Your Company a Bowl Of Carrots?

For example, when companies have not identified their target market, they are like a simple bowl of carrots, very plain and boring. Yes, if I was starving and this bowl of carrots was the only thing left on earth, I would eat some carrots. They wouldn't be my first choice, and you better believe I'm not paying a premium for them.

You see, the bowl of carrots is boring, and with the amount of options your target market has to choose from, you must stand out. When you try and please everyone, you will please no one.

Would the vast amount of the population eat the carrots if it was their only option? Sure, but again, not their first choice. You must be someone's first choice; if not, your business is in a terrifying position.

Not only are these companies walking bowls of plain, boring carrots, they expect some magic marketing formula to be able to convince people that they should choose this over what the person really wants. Do you think this is even possible? No way.

When you identify your target market, you will be excluding a massive group of people that might, maybe, one day, buy your products. Remember, only might buy your products; most likely, you will be their last option. This is a good thing. We want to first dominate a single target market, then expand. Build a massively loyal following in a select market you choose, not one that is selected for you, then expand into new markets knowing that your loyal customers will follow you through thick and thin.

An excellent example of this is Apple. When they first formed, they simply made computers, that's it. They understood who their target market was and spoke to "The Crazy Ones." They excluded a large segment of potential clientele, but they didn't care. They built a loyal following that they knew would follow them wherever they went. On the other hand, companies like Dell and HP didn't take the time to identify their target market, and didn't want to exclude anyone that might, maybe one day, want to buy their products. Compared to Apple, Dell, and HP are just simple bowls of plain carrots.

Instead of being everyone's last option, be a few's first option.

Another key benefit of choosing your target market is that you will become the expert in the field you chose and charge what you want to charge, instead of competing solely on price. You are not a jack of all trades. You are the expert, and experts charge what they want.

Focusing on your hedgehog concept

Defining your target market means you can focus on one thing and be the best in the world at it. In Jim Collins best-selling book Good To Great, he explains the importance of finding and understanding your hedgehog concept.

"Are you a hedgehog, or a fox? The fox knows many things, but the hedgehog knows one big thing. The fox is a cunning creature, able to devise a myriad of complex strategies for sneak attacks upon the hedgehog. Day in and day out, the fox circles around the hedgehog's den, waiting for the perfect moment to pounce. Fast, sleek, beautiful, fleet of foot, and crafty—the fox looks like a sure winner. The hedgehog, on the other hand, is a dowdier creature, looking like a mixup between a porcupine and a small armadillo. He waddles along, going about his simple day, searching for lunch and taking care of his home.

The fox waits in cunning silence at the juncture in the trail. The hedgehog, minding his own business, wanders right into the path of the fox. 'Aha, I've got you now' thinks the fox. He leaps out, bounding across the ground, lighting fast. The little hedgehog, sensing danger, looks up and thinks 'Here we go again. Will he ever learn?" Rolling up into a perfect little ball, the hedgehog becomes a sphere of sharp spikes, pointing outward in all directions. The fox, bounding toward his prey, sees the hedgehog defense and calls off the attack.

Retreating back to the forest, the fox begins to calculate a new line of attack. Each day, some version of this battle between the hedgehog and the fox takes place, and despite the greater cunning of the fox, the hedgehog always wins."

Most companies these days are like the fox. They have plenty of tools and tactics, but they do not have one simple quality that they are best at. Unlike the hedgehog, that can fend off almost all attacks with one simple move.

When you can define your target market and deploy all of your assets and resources to helping this particular group of people, you can be just like the hedgehog. Choose your target market, and be the best in the world at one thing. If your company is more like the fox, take a step back and understand what your business can be the best in the world and then choose the market that falls within that service.

Some of the most outstanding companies in the world are more like hedgehogs. They're simple, dowdy creatures that know "one big thing" and stick to it. Most companies, on the other hand, are more like foxes. They're crafty, cunning creatures that know many things but lack constancy. Does a heart specialist charge more than a general doctor? You bet, but you will gladly pay more for the heart specialist because you know he will give you the best answer.

Now that you understand the importance of choosing your target market let's break down how to choose one for your business.

There are two main factors that you will use when identifying your target market. The first factor is the amount of potential clientele in the marketplace, and the second factor is the return on investment you will generate from this particular market.

Let's say you own a conference center. You look at the past three years of all of the clients you have hosted, and you notice that business conferences bring, on average, 70-80% more profit than all of the other events.

Upon this finding, you decide to target people that influence the decision-making process on where to have their business conferences. Your Target Market Profile might look like this.

Business Conference Target Market Profile:

1. Owner/CEO/Event Coordinator of Company
2. Size of Company: $4,000,000 + a year
3. Employee Size: 40+
4. City: Kansas City and surrounding area
5. Event with Highest ROI: Two-day seminars

Now that your target market is determined, you can now filter out all of the other events and focus solely on the business conferences. You can design a landing page and spend all of your marketing dollars dominating this corner of the market.

Your conference center is "The Best Place To Have Business Conferences!" You are simply the best of the best for business conferences, and everyone knows it. This, in turn, will enable you to work less but make more.

To bring in consistent results from your marketing campaign, you must consistently communicate the right message to your target market. Your target market must also associate themselves with you.

Your target market has unique struggles and problems that you can solve; all you need to do is identify and communicate them. If you cannot point to your target market and say, "That is my target market, this is their struggle, and this is how I solve their problems. I am an expert in this field, and I am their best option." You will be another company in the background, a commodity. This is the worst place you can be if you are trying to grow your company.

A common misconception that I run into a lot is that my clients think their target market is a particular person. This is not correct. Your target market is who you serve; each person's individual qualities don't matter as much. All that matters is that they have unique problems that you can solve. Most of your target market will share some of the same qualities when you boil it down, but remember, as long as this person has unique problems that you can solve, they are in your target market.

Chapter Two: Identify The Target Market

To help you get an idea of who your target market is and what they want to hear, answer these questions:

1. What websites do they visit?
2. What is their #1 problem they struggle with that your product/service fixes?
3. What are their hobbies? 4. What makes them tick?
4. What keeps them up at night?
5. What is this person's day like?
6. What are they afraid of?
7. What are they angry about?
8. Who are they angry at?
9. Magazines they read?
10. What is the one thing they wish they could fix?

For example, let's say your target market is beagle owners. The answers above would look a lot like this:

1. What websites do they visit? https://www.beaglesunlimited.com/
2. What are their hobbies? Going to dog parks, taking beagles on walks, burning beagle's energy.
3. What are they afraid of? Something hurting their beagles, especially if it is hard to detect.

You get the point here. Try and step into your target market's mind and understand who they are and what is important to them.

Write down a few answers to the previous questions:

_____
_____
_____
_____
_____

With the Vending Machine Marketing Plan, it is critical to pinpoint your target market and truly understand them. If we are not 100% sure about who you are trying to reach, there is no way we will create a message that will genuinely resonate with them. Without our target market identified, the entire campaign will be too generic, and the whole marketing campaign will be a complete waste.

We want to make sure you are a big fish in a small pond. Without truly understanding where your pond is, you will be a small fish in a massive ocean, and no one will recognize you. Instead, if you start out dominating your small pond and understanding the long-term strategic view, you will be able to master the largest of oceans.

Look at one of the most successful companies in the world, Amazon. The first thing they did was focus on serving one target market, book readers. They solved a common problem that every book reader faced, the book they wanted was not in stock at their local book store. Amazon solved that. Once they dominated this sector, they expanded to CD's, DVD's, and kept growing and growing to the massive company they are today.

Chapter Two: Identify The Target Market

Jeff Bezos understands that first, you must dominate one single marketplace, then expand. One step at a time, with patience and persistence. Today, Amazon is more than an eCommerce behemoth. With AWS and all of the recent acquisitions they have made, you simply never would have guessed that they started by dominating one market. Book readers.

Let's look at a real-world example. One of my clients owns a plumbing business, and after I introduced this idea to him, he started taking notice of the clientele that was the most profitable. He had three key categories of clients that he currently served:

Contractors

1. Commercial Clients
2. Residential

After looking at his past clients, he found the jackpot.

His target market was tight-knit communities in the older parts of town. They refer him to all of their neighbors, and they always have plenty of work for him to do. We took the time and figured out who was actually making the call, and notice it was almost always a female. Of course! The wife always is the one making the decisions around the house! I pulled out a looseleaf piece of paper and jotted down his target market profile.

Target Clientele Profile:

1. Residential Homes $350,000+
2. In XYZ Part Of Town
3. Married Women
4. Ages 35-60
5. 20+ year-old homes

This target market calls him more often, refers him to all of their neighbors and friends, and has more work for him to do than any other job. It's a no brainer. Now that we have a complete understanding of who we are creating our message for, we will have no problem completely dominating this corner of the market.

Just because you are focusing on this corner of the market does not mean you cannot take other jobs and create side marketing plans. I encourage this. Once you have outgrown your initial pond, continue to level up and dominate more and more of the available market. Keep growing until you can eventually dominate an entire ocean. Always take one step at a time, and start by dominating one single pond.

Chapter Two: Identify The Target Market

Take some time to jot down your Target Market Profile so we can refer back to it throughout this book. Now that you have your target clientele identified, we will start constructing the message to persuade and influence your target market and get them to use your company!

Your Target Market Profile Sheet

_____
_____
_____
_____
_____
_____
_____
_____

CHAPTER THREE: INFLUENCING TARGET MARKET

Now that we understand who our target market is, what we need to do is truly understand how we will influence them to use your company. Once you understand this fundamental aspect of marketing, every advertisement you create will provide outstanding results, so let's jump right in!

In 2016, a company singlehandedly changed the course of the United States Presidential Election by simply understanding who their target market was and how to influence them. Luckily for you, there will be no need to set up highly illegal data harvesting methods to identify your target market because we have already created our Target Market Profile!

First, we will look at how Cambridge Analytica harvested data to identify their target market. Then we will examine the incredible way they were able to influence and persuade their target market. Who was their target market you ask? Undecided voters.

They examined data from the individual's Facebook profile, identified the ones that were still undecided on who they were going to vote for, and created ads that would influence them to vote for their party instead of the opposition.

They analyzed individual's Facebook profiles and put them in categories based on their online identity. What sites they visited, what they watched, what articles they read, the purchases they made, and so on. In each category, they would create specific ads that would persuade and influence the individual to vote for a particular candidate based on their online tendencies.

The first step they made sure to complete was identifying who their target market was. They knew if they didn't have a complete understanding of their target market and who they were trying to persuade, their marketing campaign would be a complete waste.

For example, if an individual showed online tendencies that they were big on border security, Cambridge Analytica would run advertisements to reinforce this belief. They would show all of the critical benefits of why they needed a secure border based on emotions, not logic. Look at the way politicians describe border security. One hundred percent based on emotions. They know if they used logic, their message would fall on deaf ears.

After their target market was identified, they took the time to understand how to influence them by comparing their data with the eight basic human desires that every single human is instilled with at birth.

In this chapter, we will focus on how to persuade your target market to use your company over your competitors.

Chapter Three: Influencing Target Market

I will break down the exact method to use so you can influence your target market correctly.

If Cambridge Analytica was able to use this method to influence a United States Presidential Election, then I can almost guarantee it will work for you. Remember, the technique Cambridge Analytica used to identify their target market was illegal. Not the method they used to influence their target market. In no way do I condone the massively illegal operation that they set up.

The first step we need to take when trying to influence our target market is to understand how the mind works and how to influence it. You see, the human brain has three major levels, and it is our job to know which level to reach and how to reach it. If we are unable to do so, then all of our marketing campaigns will be a waste.

Brain evolution

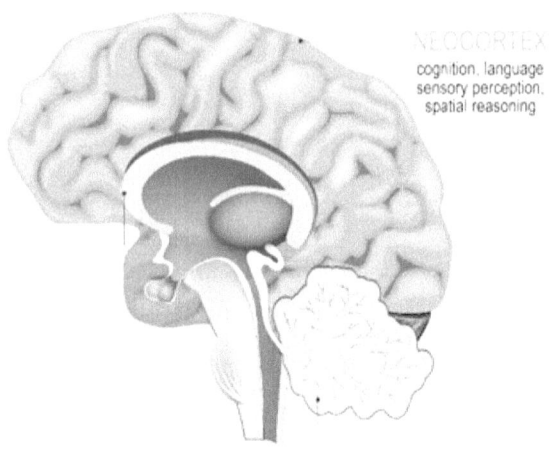

33

Starting with the newest level of our brain, the neocortex. This part of the brain is in charge of analytical thought and language. It can understand complicated information, like facts and figures, but does not drive behavior.

Most of the companies that are running advertisements focus on the neocortex. They focus on all of the logical reasons someone should use their company—things like price, and warranty to name a couple.

Limbic system

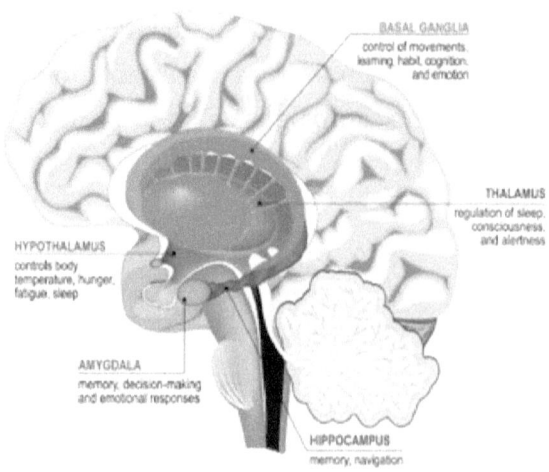

The middle two sections comprise the limbic brain. The limbic brain is responsible for all of our feelings, such as trust and security. It is also responsible for most human behavior and decision-making but has no capacity for rational thought or language.

This part of the brain can sense when danger is coming, even though you cannot explain why. "Gut feelings" or just being completely sold on a product or person without genuinely understanding the reason is your limbic brain at work. This is the part of the brain that helped humans evolve as a species.

This chapter is all about understanding how to bypass the neocortex and communicate directly to the limbic part of the brain. No matter how much money you spend on marketing or how much time you spend on creating your keyword list, if your ads communicate to the neocortex instead of the limbic part of the brain, all of your campaigns will flop. You can make sure that your company always produces the right message by creating a Key Human Driver Statement.

Here are the eight ways you will be able to get in touch with the limbic brain. Choose which one your business satisfies. Below is what Drew Eric Whitman calls "Life Force 8!" in his bestselling book, Cashvertising.

1. Survival, enjoyment of life, life extension
2. Enjoyment of food and beverages
3. Freedom from fear, pain, and danger
4. Sexual companionship
5. Comfortable living conditions
6. To be superior, winning, keeping up with the Joneses
7. Care and protection of loved ones
8. Social approval

You must step back and ask yourself, at the most basic level, what does my company do?

1. Does your company create products that help people live a longer, heather life?
2. Does your company give people freedom from fear, pain, or danger?
3. Does your company help people feel superior?
4. Does your company provide care and protection for loved ones?
5. Does your company help your clients get social approval?
6. Does your product help your clients get sexual companionship? (This is a huge one! If you can link your business back to this in any way, do it!)
7. Does your company help people live comfortably?

Remember, your Key Human Driver Statement is just your guide to reaching the limbic part of the brain. All of the marketing pieces that we create will link back to this simple message to ensure that we speak to the limbic part of the brain, not the neocortex. We will never put out an advertisement that says, "My company XYZ will help you enjoy freedom from fear, pain, and danger!"

For example, people don't buy insurance. They buy freedom from fear, pain, or danger! People do not buy a Rolex to tell the time. It's a statement. It's keeping up with the Joneses or being superior! Every business solves human desire. We need to identify the human desire that you fulfill, so later on down the road, we can build off of it to create our marketing campaigns.

Let's step back and look at another example of how

Cambridge Analytica was able to completely change the entire course of an election with a single basic human desire. In the Netflix documentary The Great Hack, they show the exact sales pitch Alexander Nix used to show how they looked at problems and interfered with the election in Trinidad. During this section, try and identify which one of the eight desires they used.

"There are two main political parties, one for blacks, one for the Indians. And you know, they screw each other. So, we were working for the Indians. We went to the client and said, 'we want to target the youth.' And we try and increase apathy. The campaign had to be non-political because the kids don't care about politics. It had to be reactive because they are lazy. So we came up with this campaign, which was all about: Be part of a gang. Do something cool. Be part of a movement. And it was called the "Do So!" Campaign. It means 'I'm not going to vote.'

'Do so! Don't vote.' It's a sign of resistance against, not the government, against politics and voting. They are making their own YouTube videos. They spray painted the prime minister's house with 'Do So!' It was carnage.

We knew that when it came to voting, all the Afro-Caribbean kids wouldn't vote because of the Do So. But all of the Indian kids would do what their parents told them to do, which is go out and vote. They had a lot of fun doing this, but they're not going to go against their parents' will. The difference in 18-to-35-year-old turnout was like 40%. That swung the election about 6%, which was all we needed in a very close election."

In no way do I condone Cambridge Analytica's action

in any sense. I really just want you to understand how effective these methods are when used correctly.

So how were they able to influence an entire generation not to vote? "Be part of a gang. Do something cool. Be part of a movement. And it was called the "Do So!" Campaign. It means "I'm not going to vote."

These kids wanted social approval from their peers, to fit in, and it worked. Kids especially want to fit in with the crowd and make new friends. The opinions of others mean a lot. Cambridge Analytica understood this and used it to get the results they were looking for.

What if your company doesn't fit within the LF8 framework? Don't worry. There are nine learned human desires that you can use. These are not as effective as the LF8 in reaching the limbic part of the brain, but they are better than nothing.

The 9 Learned or Secondary wants are:

1. To be informed
2. Curiosity
3. Cleanliness of body and surroundings
4. Efficiency
5. Convenience
6. Dependability / Quality
7. Expression of beauty and style
8. Economy/profit
9. Bargains

Life Force 8 are basic needs that are programmed in us at birth, and if you can, stick to those.

If there is absolutely no way you can fit your business into the LF8, use these secondary drivers.

After writing down your Key Human Driver Statement and taking the time to truly understand why your business satisfies this basic desire, you are one step closer to completely dominating your industry. Once you have identified your target market and understand how to speak directly to the limbic part of the brain responsible for all decision making, I want you to write this statement out and put it where you can see it every day. Your life will truly change when you can plant your feet firmly into the ground and say...

Key Human Driver Statement

My Company serves_____
(Target Market) to ensure that they _____,
(Life Force Eight Desire) and I will make sure that my
target market will be able to identify with this message in
everything I do!

Now that you have a solid grasp on this concept, take notice of which advertisements actually speak to the part of your brain that drives decision making. On average, I will only see one or two advertisements out of the hundreds that I see daily that are set up correctly and talk to the limbic brain. The rest are simply garbage.

Reminder: no one will see this except you and your marketing team. This is just the starting point that all of your advertising campaigns will stem from! This whole point of this process is so that you will always be able to come back and check and make sure that one, we are focusing on our target market and two, it is speaking directly to their limbic part of their brain.

Throughout this book, we will continue to reference this statement to ensure that the advertisements we create will fit our Key Human Driver Statement.

To recap:

Humans are very emotional creatures. We need to make sure that we understand the underlying emotions that influence every decision we make. The Life Force 8 is your golden ticket to bypass the neocortex and communicate directly to the limbic part of the brain.

By now, you should have a complete understanding of which basic desire your company solves. For the rest of this book, we will focus on how to communicate this message to your target market to generate massive amounts of clientele for your business.

This will be the cheat sheet to ensure your company is creating the best advertisements in your industry.

All of the necessary components are:

- Target Market Profile
- Key Human Driver Statement

Key Human Driver Statement

My Company serves_____
(Target Market) to ensure that they _____,
(Life Force Eight Desire) and I will make sure that my target market will be able to identify with this message in everything I do!

CHAPTER FOUR: UNDERSTANDING THE BASICS OF DIGITAL MARKETING

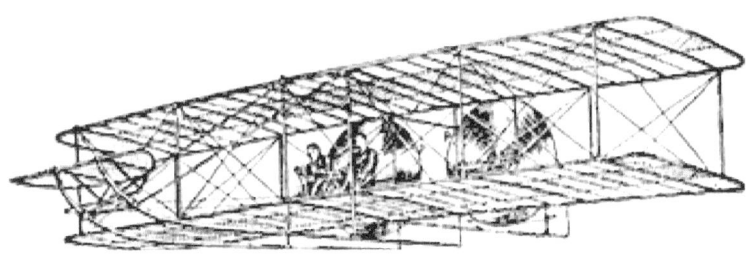

I n 1903, there was a race to see who could build the first flying machine. As most people are unaware, the Wright brothers were not the only ones trying to achieve this goal. Samuel Pierpont Langley was a well-financed inventor who was competing with the Wright Brothers. "Langley was focused on power, and the image of an arrow shot through the air: put enough force behind the machine, and it would fly."

Langley and his mechanics felt ready to test the aerodrome. On October 7, 1903, pilot and chief mechanic Charles Manly climbed aboard the craft, mounted to the top of a houseboat on the Potomac. Reporters swarmed to the site. A catapult launched the aerodrome, and it crashed straight into the river. A reporter said it flew "like a handful of mortar." Simply put, their model of "strap a big enough engine on, and it will fly" failed miserably.

On the other hand, the Wright brothers had a different approach. They understood that they needed to solve three fundamental problems if they wanted to fly: liftoff, balance, and power. Before they even introduced a massive motor, they focused on just getting it to glide, then added the motor, not the other way around!

Most companies take the Langley approach and think that if they throw enough money at marketing, it will generate results, but it won't. This chapter is all about making sure our online presence can glide so that later we can strap on massive engines without failure.

These are the simple building blocks that you need to know before launching your marketing campaign. You must take the time to understand and implement the tactical steps to grow your company. What we will be doing in this chapter is establishing a foundation for our online presence. Without a proper foundation, we will not be able to run campaigns and ultimately convert prospects into clientele.

Just like how the Wright brothers understood their essential components, here are ours. The Big Four we need to establish are Facebook,

Google My Business, Local SEO, and your business Website. Once you understand the basics of each of these critical platforms, we will be able to create the campaigns and bring in massive amounts of clientele.

Facebook

Before we talk about Facebook's technicalities, I want to make sure you understand how you need to approach this platform. Believe it or not, there is a specific way you need to handle Facebook so that you can grow your page and get introduced to new clientele. Later on, I will talk about running campaigns on Facebook, but for now, it is all about setting up your page correctly so that you can glide.

What is the best way to approach Facebook? Think of it this way. Facebook is a place where people escape from reality, a place to relax, a place to socialize and catch up with friends. You need to treat it like you are at a party.

Let's imagine for a minute you are going to a party to catch up with some friends that you haven't seen in a long time. Assuming that you are like me, the first thing I am going to do is to make sure I look as presentable as possible. Pick out an outfit, get a haircut, all the basics to ensure I am looking my best. It simply does not make sense to show up looking like you just rolled out of bed, right? This is the first step to making sure your Facebook page is contributing to the end goal is making sure it is aesthetically pleasing.

Now that I have the perfect outfit, I head out the door to go to the party. I am more than excited to be able to catch up with old friends. When I arrive, I greet all of my friends and grab a drink from the bar. Out of the corner of my eye, I spot one of my old buddies I used to play soccer with and ask him how he is doing. Rather than telling me about his wife and kids, he starts pitching me on his services that he is currently selling.

After he gets done, I tell him to give me a call later. I then say to him that I am just trying to relax and catch up with some old buddies. Now I know this sounds farfetched, but this is how you need to treat Facebook. Do not try and sell to people that are just trying to relax. Focus on building relationships instead.

When we get to the section on postings, I will explain how to approach this situation, so you don't confuse and scare off potential clientele.

The Facebook Page Makeover

Humans process images faster than we do words, so our Facebook profile must be pleasing to the eye. The first thing you need to do is make sure that your Facebook page has a logo, and it is sized correctly. Your logo is your brand, and you must do everything in your power to make sure that it always looks clean and neat. If your logo looks substandard, ask whoever made the logo to size it for your Business Facebook Page profile picture. If you cannot get in touch with the person who created your logo, reach out to my team, and we will make you one for free.

We need to make sure we are using the space in our header to either promote a product or service or show off previous work. For WiseGuys, we have one of the promotional videos we took for one of our clients.

If you are going to use a photo for your header, the best way to utilize the space is to promote deals your company is having or an upcoming event your company is hosting. Ensure you have the correct dimensions of the header so it isn't cut off or wonky. Use the platform canva.com to create your headers. They already have prebuilt templates with the custom dimensions; you can edit them and add your logo. I'll refer back to canva.com later when discussing social media posting.

After you finish your logo and header, the next step is to make sure the information on your Facebook page is filled out and correct. Facebook has spots where you will fill in different information for your company, as in the correct URL for your business website, your business's physical location, industry, phone number, etc.

This is important for making sure Facebook is helping your business rank higher on Google. When all of your business information is the same across the internet, that is when you start ranking higher in the local map packs.

Remember that Facebook's critical aspect is not bringing in a massive amount of clientele on its own. The main job of your Facebook Business Page is to build on top of all of the other tools we will use later on in this book. That being said, I want to show you the best ways to post on Facebook so that you have a greater chance of getting in front of potential prospects.

Posting For Greatness

What is the main goal we need to focus on to ensure success on Facebook? Interactions.

Without interactions, Facebook will not let your post

Chapter Four: Understanding The Basics Of Digital Marketing

see the light of day. The more interactions you get, the more people will see your post.

Here are the best ways to get people to interact with your post. The key methods are:

1. Sentimental Posts. Posts of kittens or puppies, posts of kids, posts about a charitable cause.
2. Utility. Post that explains "How to do" stuff, especially things that are counter-intuitive or funny.
3. Funny. Humor is big on Facebook. Posting jokes, funny quotes, videos, images. Anything to get people to laugh.
4. Surveys, polls, contests. Ask your audience a question, and getting them to use the comments to answer will generate a lot of interaction. A great way to generate a lot of comments is asking a trivia question, and the first person to answer the question correctly gets a prize of some sort!
5. Quotes. Sentimental, humorous, make you think quotes
6. Giveaways. As an example, "Like this post to be entered for a chance to win a $25 Amazon Gift Card!"

One of the first things I do when creating a plan for my client's Facebook page is to see what their competitors are doing and improve on it. What do they have for their header? Is their logo clean in their profile picture? What posts get the most interaction? You're not just copying what they are doing; you are observing and improving.

If you notice that every time they post something about their employee of the month, they get a good amount of interaction, you need to use that and improve on it. How? One example off the top of my head would be Employee Pet of the Month? Or Customer Pet of the Month?

You should never, ever, just copy and paste a post from your competitor. Take their idea and create something completely new and original from it. We need to look at Facebook as a place where people relax and escape from reality, and your job is to assist them with that. We just want eyes on your brand, simple as that. Later on in this book, I will show you how to bring on clients with this platform, but for now, I want you to focus on entertaining them!

See a funny post about a dog? Share it on your Business Facebook Page. Exciting article about your industry? Share it. You might be asking yourself, "Can I ever post about my business?" Of course, you can! It's important not to overload your target prospects with boring information that they couldn't give two cents about. My rule of thumb is to use the 80/20 rule. For every four posts, you can create one self-promoting post.

Below is a list of my favorite posting ideas, make them your own, and expand on them! Make sure you also find a way to infuse them to get the best interactions for your business. Remember when I talked about Canva.com earlier? This is another instance where Canva can help you out a lot for creating eye-catching posts.

Chapter Four: Understanding The Basics Of Digital Marketing

1. Ask questions, and start discussions. (Do you like…? Are you a fan of…?)
2. Tell your story or a story of one of your customers
3. Dig into problems that you solve
4. Post on holidays (including "holidays" such as National Taco Day!)
5. Promote products or services
6. Share a special offer
7. Show customers enjoying your products and services
8. Client testimonials
9. Show off product features with infographics
10. Share inspirational quotes in picture form
11. Funny images
12. Share hints, tips, and tutorial
13. Show behind the scenes
14. Highlight your charitable side
15. Share popular meme
16. Jump on fads in popular culture
17. Add snack-sized data
18. Post about what is trending
19. Expert Tips
20. Snippets from your blog
21. Throw Back Thursdays
22. Post a poll
23. Business books
24. How-to guides
25. Infographics
26. Ask followers about business decisions

Try to post videos at least once a week with the ideas I shared with you above. Videos are essential to connect with your followers and build a real connection. Your video does not need to be extremely long, nor does it have to be professional. Most cameras that come with most smartphones these days have more than enough quality to create a short video of yourself.

When to post

The question that I always get asked is "When is the best time to post?" and for a while, it was indeed up in the air, but now, Facebook has made it easy for us to see when it is the best time to post for our industry with Audience Insights. Not only does it give you the best time to post, but what days of the week to post, and what content is the most popular.

Chapter Four: Understanding The Basics Of Digital Marketing

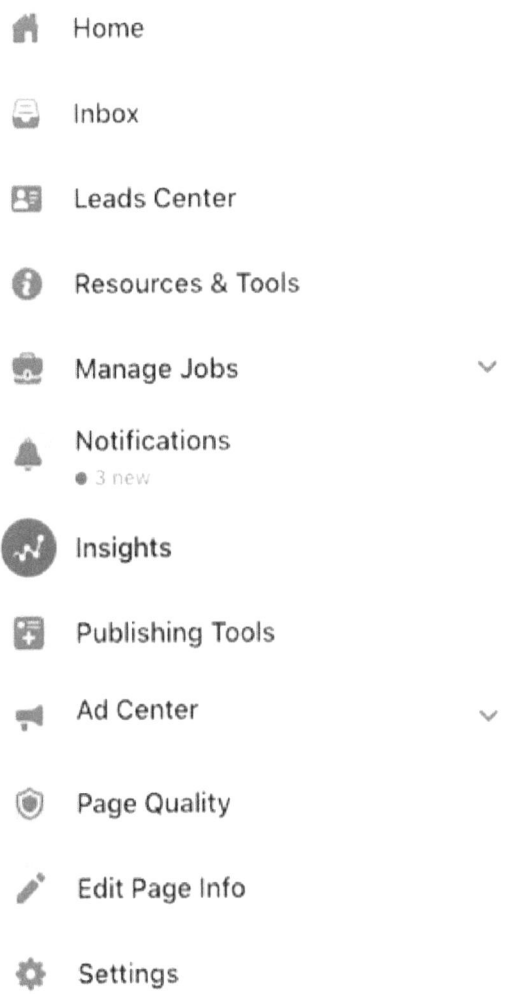

Facebook is a crucial foundational block that will generate massive results for your business when we start our marketing campaigns. Make sure your Facebook page is correctly set up and is aesthetically pleasing. Post like you're at a party, and don't walk around pitching people that are just trying to have a good time!

Google My Business

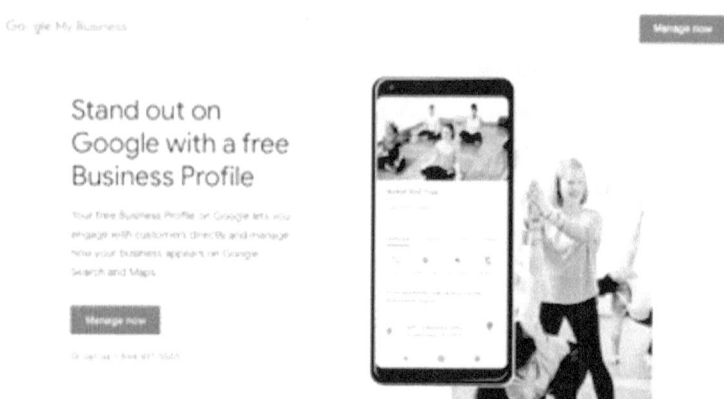

Another foundational block to establishing your online presence is Google My Business. Before we hop into the technicalities of GMB, we must understand why it was created and what purpose it serves.

Google My Business is a free tool that helps you manage how your business appears on

Google Search and Maps. This free profile enables you to add your business name, address, business hours, services you prove, and reply and monitor customer reviews.

When you are searching for a business in your city, most likely, what will pull up is a bunch of Google My Business listings. For businesses that operate in a defined area, this is vital to your success. Let's hop into optimizing your Google My Business Profile.

The Key Qualities To GMB

When it comes to GMB, consistency is a significant key to your success. Make sure your GMB information is the same information that is used on your website and all other social media to build NAP citations to ensure you rank higher in local SEO. (More on this later)

The first thing you must do is make sure that you have either claimed or created a Google My Business profile. If your business already has a Google My Business profile, but it is not claimed, you need to make sure you do this immediately. The way you will find out if it is claimed or not is by simply searching for your business on Google.

If a profile has already been created but not claimed, it will have a link that will say "Own This Business?" Click on this link, and it will have you verify that you own the business in one of two ways. The first way will be by calling your business line. The second way is by sending a postcard to your business address in the mail.

If you do not already have a profile created, you will search Google My Business in the search bar, and most likely, it will be the first link that comes up. Once you are on the actual website, you will follow the prompts on creating your GMB profile. They will likely send you a postcard, and you will have to wait for it to arrive to complete the rest of these steps.

Now that you have either claimed or created your Google My Business profile, we will focus on the key technical aspects that will provide the best results for your company. Out of all of the basic building blocks, this is the most important for bringing on new clientele.

Business Information

When you first log in to your profile, Google will walk you through the steps of adding basic information about your business. When you're doing this, make sure the information you are putting into your profile matches your Website and Facebook. If not, Google will tax your ranking greatly. Always make sure your name, address, and phone number are correct across the web. Also referred to as NAP, this is Google's factchecker, so ensure all of this information lines up with all of your other profiles.

Google will give you a score for how complete your profile is.

Complete your listing

Improve your local search ranking and help your customers with a complete profile

@ Add profile short name +

Once you have added your basic information, you will move on to choosing your business category. Google will make you choose one top-level category that describes your business. Another critical key to this process is that

Chapter Four: Understanding The Basics Of Digital Marketing

you must select from the categories they already have prebuilt; you cannot create your own category.

After you have selected your category, you need to make sure you add secondary categories. Add as many secondary categories that can apply to your business.

After this is completed, you need to make sure you scroll down and fill in the services you provide and the products you sell. Make sure that you add as many as you can.

After you have completed the basic information and added the industry and services you provide, you need to define where you do business. Add all of the cities that you would like to show up in. This isn't guaranteeing you will, but you will have a greater chance to do so when you add the different locations.

Once all of the information for your Google My Business is filled in, we can move onto Posting and Generating Reviews.

Photos and Postings

Now that you have added all of the basic information, you will now need to add your logo and other photos to your Google My Business profile. There will be a list on the left-hand side of the page marked photos. Once you click that, it will prompt you to upload your logo, cover photo, and any other photos you think your target clientele will want to see. The more you can add, the better. Add photos of your previous work, work vans, inside your office or store, happy clients, anything that you feel is important. Remember, looks are everything. Make sure you can put as many good photos as you can.

Posting on your Google My Business can be a bit more sales-oriented than Facebook, and here is why. Facebook is a social media platform designed to connect friends and family. Your Google My Business profile is a place where people are going to decide which company to use. For Google My Business posts, you want to focus primarily on promoting your business and sales that your business is having.

These posts only last for a certain amount of time, so you can be more direct with Google posts, such as: „This weekend we are having a 30% off sale! Come in!"

Reputation Management

This is one of the essential parts of this whole book when it comes to generating clients. Google My Business is one of the single most important places to make sure you have a plethora of fivestar reviews. What's the best way to get them from your clients?

On Google My Business, there is a section that says, "share your business profile." This will generate a link that you can send to your customers to leave a review with the least amount of effort possible.

Chapter Four: Understanding The Basics Of Digital Marketing

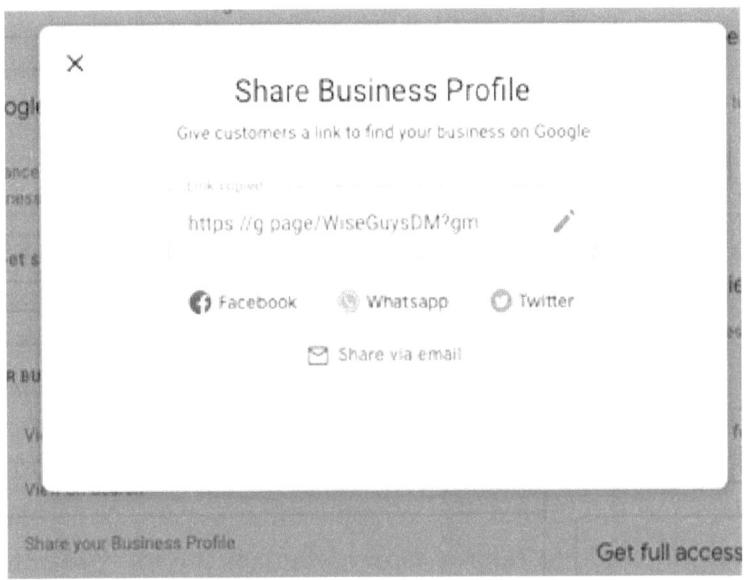

The key here is to make sure that you are making it as easy as possible for your client to write a review. Reviews are not only crucial for ranking your business on the search engines, but it also establishes social proof and wins the trust of your target market. More and more people trust online reviews to decide which business they will choose, so you must take this very seriously. On average, my clients with 50 or more five-star reviews on Google have a conversion rate of at least triple of the clients with less than 50 five-star reviews. That being said, do not take getting reviews as a side task. This needs to be one of your business's key milestones that you track and keep a continuing tally on.

Now, no matter what, you will get one or two upset clients, and that is alright. Some people might have unrealistic expectations of what your business can do or what you can provide. So whenever you get a one-star review, the first thing you must do is ask yourself, "what can we learn from this?" and "was this avoidable?" If so, reach out and try and make the situation right. If not, simply reply to the review through your Google My Business Profile.

Ensure when you are replying to their review that you are respectful and polite and explain the situation and how you did everything possible to fix the situation. After this, let it go and move on.

Google My Business is a fantastic tool for your business. You need to make sure that you are using it correctly. We understand the basics of what the profile should look like and the importance of generating reviews. But what are the tools to help it rank higher on the local search engines? Glad you asked. But before we break the amazing world of Local Search Engine Optimization (SEO), remember this one thing: your Google My Business Profile is the number one factor for ranking high for Local SEO, so take your time and make sure your GMB is solid!

Local SEO

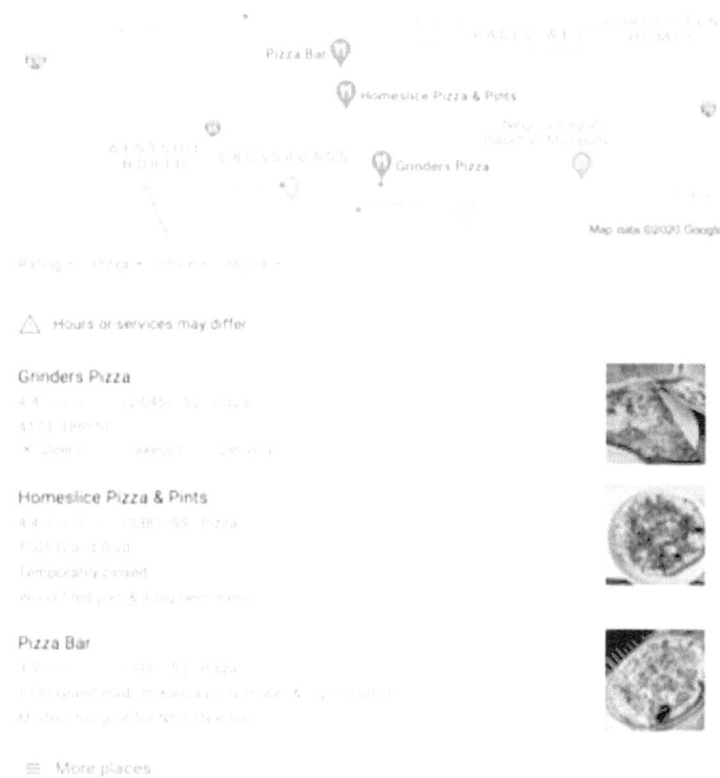

Local SEO is vital for almost every business because nearly 46% of Google searches are done with local intent, meaning that people are looking for products and services in their city. Also, the term "Near me" has grown 150 percent faster than traditional search terms. (Google)

We need to make sure we are doing everything we can to rank high in the local map pack. We have already completed two steps in the process (Facebook and Google My Business.) It's time to break it down even further. I am going to give you the basic tools and strategies so that you can dominate Local SEO.

Google has a different set of ranking factors that determine the result that it will pull up for local searches. Below are the different sets that Google uses to rank your local listing.

1. The location that the person is searching from
2. Name, address, and Phone citations
3. Presence of Google My Business listing
4. Keywords used in Google My Business profile
5. The sentiment of online reviews
6. Keywords used in online reviews
7. Number of "check-ins" at that location
8. Shares on social media

The first factor on our list is "the location that the person is searching from."

This is the most fundamental characteristic of Local SEO. When you are looking for a Pizza restaurant to go to, you are not interested in seeing results from Seattle if you are in Kansas City. When you search for "Pizza Near Me," you will get the closest pizza joints.

The second factor on the list is "NAP Citations." Like I stated briefly in the section prior, NAP stands for name, address, and phone number for your business. Why is this important? You see, this is how Google confirms that all of your business information is correct. The more often they see the NAP citations, the more confident they are with promoting your business. That is why it is crucial to get consistent NAP citations on as many reputable websites as you can! A few websites include Facebook, Yelp, and Google My Business. Tools that will help identify and fix NAP listings are tools like BrightLocal.com or Moz.com.

The Third and Fourth Factor on our list is Presence of Google My Business listing and the Keywords used in Google My Business profile. We completed this step earlier in this chapter, so all is good here.

The Fifth Factor on our list is "The Sentiment of Online Reviews." Now you might be wondering, "why are reviews so important to have?" Here is why. Over 15.4% of the way Google Ranks you is based on how many reviews you have and what rating they are. If you have no reviews or a bunch of one-star reviews, you are simply not going to rank as high.

Like I said above, not only is this going to hurt your ranking, but people simply won't use a business with a bunch of one-star reviews. Build up your reputation and ranking with reviews!

The Sixth Factor on our list is "Keywords used in Online Reviews." What does that mean? For example, if you are a pizza restaurant in Kansas City, a perfect review would look like, "ABC Pizza here in Kansas City is the best! Cannot wait to come back!" Whenever possible, try and get your client to include the city and primary keywords you want to rank for!

The Seventh Factor on our list is "Number of check-ins at the location." This can happen on pretty much any social media site or Google.

For example, there is a health club by my house that offers 10% off to people that check-in via their Facebook page. With this method, they get views from the person's

Facebook friends, which helps them rank higher on local searches. Smart.

The Eighth Factor is "Shares on Social Media." This is also why it is crucial to post content and information on your Facebook page that your target market will interact with and share.

What do you think is the most important factor that Google uses when ranking businesses online? Google My Business signals. That is why it is important to make sure you take the time and show your GMB profile a lot of attention. Generate a massive amount of reviews and continuously update and add photos to your GMB profile.

Always remember, Google is notorious for changing the qualities they look for when ranking sites. Make sure you are checking to make sure the information in this section is accurate and will help you rank higher on Google For Local Searches.

Your Website

The fourth basic tool that we need to understand is your website's role in your overall marketing strategy. One of the most common questions I get from my clients is, "what makes a good website?"

Now, before I answer this question, I always hit them with a follow-up question. "What are you looking to get out of it?" You see, what makes a good website is having it achieve what it was created to do. If you created a website to generate leads, and for some reason, never generates leads, then the website sucks!

Your site needs to have a purpose, and once you have

identified that purpose, you can build a site around that. When you just want to show off previous work, client testimonials, and services you provide, there is simply no need to buy a massively expensive website. (Later on in this book, I will talk about the qualities that make a remarkable landing page to convert traffic from your advertisements we run.)

Another good way to look at your website is your online storefront. These days so much research is done online that you must make sure that your website is something you are proud of. You would never let a potential client come into your office or storefront when it is disgusting; make sure they don't see an outdated or absent website!

Education

What do I mean by education? Your website needs to be packed with valuable information that shows your target market that you are an expert in your industry. Creating a blog or videos is a simple and effective way to teach your target market that you know what you are talking about, but it will also help your ranking on the search engines.

I'm sure that this is not the first time hearing about the importance of blogs and educational videos, so I want to give you a few pointers that I have learned over the years.

Headlines

These are the words that count the most. Get this part wrong, and no one will want to read your blog. Buffer, an online blog site, gave some great headline strategies that are "backed by psychology." After you read this list, you will notice that some of the biggest companies use these methods on every post they publish.

They are:

1. Surprise: "This Is Not A Perfect Blog Post (But It Could've Been)"
2. Questions: "Do You Know How to Create the Perfect Blog Post?"
3. Curiosity gap: "Ten Ingredients in a Perfect Blog Post. Number 9 Is Impossible!"
4. Negatives: "Never Write a Boring Blog Post Again"
5. How to: "How to Create A Perfect Blog Post"
6. Numbers: "Ten Tips to Create The Perfect Blog Post"
7. Audience referencing: "For People on the Verge of Writing the Perfect Blog Post"
8. Specificity: "The Six-Part Process to Getting Twice the Traffic To Your Blog Post"

Once you can hook them with a headline, you must make sure that you keep them around. The first couple of sentences should be a hook that will intrigue them to stick around and read to the end.

Also, at the beginning of the blog you should keep your paragraphs around 1-3 sentences. Make it very easy to read, and have plenty of breaks to ensure the reader does not feel overwhelmed and continues to read.

Generating Ideas To Write About:

- What are some of the common questions people email you about?
- Something that frustrates you
- Industry news
- Top 10 things that you want your readers to know
- Something new you learned about your industry
- A funny story
- A new project you are working on

Another way I was able to generate ideas to write about was by asking my friends and family this question, "What questions do you have about my profession?" For example, when I asked my grandmother this question, I got enough content to write about for two or three years, at least.

SECRETS RECAP:

We are only establishing a foundation for our online presence. We understand that before we strap on massive engines, the first thing we need to do is make sure we can glide. We have taken the necessary steps to ensure success.

Remember, if we are unable to glide, we will not run effective campaigns and ultimately convert prospects into clientele.

Now, this chapter was not created to turn you into an expert on each platform. That was not the purpose. Our goal was for you to have the fundamentals down. Now you can continue to learn and upgrade your skill for each one of these platforms.

Make sure that you can glide, so that when we start our marketing campaigns, we can generate massive amounts of clientele for your business!

PART 2
IMPLEMENT THE TACTICS!

Understanding the basics of the Vending Machine Marketing Plan, and establishing its foundation is the most important part of this whole process. Without the foundation, all of the work from here on out will be a waste.

Make sure you have:

1. Established Grand Strategy
2. Identified Target Market
3. Created Your Key Human Driver Statement
4. Established The Basics For Your Online Presence
5. Now it's time to move on and start creating your company's marketing plan.

In this section, we will cover:

1. How to bait the hook to generate interest
2. Creating the actual ads and launching the campaigns
3. How to capture the leads with landing pages
4. How to convert the leads into clientele

CHAPTER FIVE: YOUR BAIT

It was a scorching hot day in the middle of August in Kansas City, Missouri. I foolishly walked to Chipotle a couple of blocks away from my office. I was a couple of steps from the front door when I got a call from one of my clients. As I looked down at the caller ID, I prepared myself for the worst. You see, this particular client wasn't necessarily sold on the way I approached marketing, so I assumed he was calling to let me know he wanted to try a new strategy.

As soon I said, "Hello," I heard a big booming voice on the end of the line yell, "YOU ARE THE MAN!"

I replied with, "Of course I am," not really sure what to say.

I then asked him what the deal was. He told me that after just three weeks after implementing this complete strategy, he had already doubled his all-time greatest month, and there was still one week left!

He continued to explain that all of the clients who

decided to use his business downloaded his Ethical Bribe (which we will cover in this chapter) and received all of his follow up emails, and decided to try him out. He said that the clients truly felt like he took the time to educate them and build a lasting relationship, rather than just sell them. Right at that moment, I knew I had hit a gold mine.

When companies are marketing themselves, they rarely understand the massive amounts of relationship building and trust that you have to achieve before the prospect uses your company. You have to make sure that you are offering something of value that your target market will want to get them to interact with your company for the first time. In this chapter, I will show you how to start the relationship off on the right foot with an Ethical Bribe.

Ethical Bribe

An Ethical Bribe is creating something that your target market would want in exchange for their name, email, and phone number. We are merely giving them something of value for their contact information.

Why go through all of this trouble, you might ask? Why not just dump garbage on them as every other company does? Here's why. Back in the days of early digital marketing, you were able just to create a Google AdWords campaign and drive people to your website and see an excellent return. It was also quite affordable, but not anymore.

Over the years, we saw a massive migration from traditional advertising to online marketing, primarily Google

Ads. As more businesses made the transition, the "clicks" grew more expensive, and the conversion rate went way down. Now anytime you go on the internet feels like you're walking in Times Square—advertisements everywhere!

Not only do you have to compete for clientele at a much more competitive rate, but you also have to make sure the people that are seeing your advertisement turn into clientele, or at least give you their contact information. If not, you'll quickly run out of marketing dollars.

Ethical Bribes also ensure that everyone clicking on your advertisements is potential clientele. If your Ethical Bribe is "The 5 Ways To Dominate On The Soccer Field," very few football players are going to click on the advertisement, saving you time and money.

Recent studies suggest that before a prospect uses your company, they must see or hear from you seven to twelve times. When you can grab their information and contact them directly, you have started that connection. You also won't have to keep paying "big tech" to get in touch with your potential clients, but more on that later.

You need to stand out from all of this competition by creating an Ethical Bribe that gives value to your target market and paints you as an expert. Something that they actually will want to read, rather than just getting boring information puked on them.

Humans are always secretly asking, "What's in it for me?" When you create an advertisement that speaks to that side of humans, you will be light years ahead of the competition rather than the typical nonsense: the more value, the better. My rule of thumb is that you need to create something you would charge around $200 for. This just ensures you are providing something of real value.

Warning: if you promise value and do not fulfill your promise, all of your credibility is lost, and you can kiss the prospect goodbye. No second date for you! Going back to being able to stand out from your competition, look at all of the marketing messages today; it is usually something that looks like this:

XYZ INC, Quality Since 1955
Services we provide:
Service A
Service B
Service C Call for a free estimate!
(Talking to my Neocortex, Snooze!)

Boring. Companies are actually spending money on advertisements that look like this? No wonder they claim marketing "doesn't work!" This is your competition, and we are going to blow their asses out of the water!

We're only asking for a second date here, not going for the home run with our advertisements. That will come later. Your strategy needs to be infused with short term tactics. When you take the time and create something that will add value to your target market's lives, that is when you move from being just another business begging for attention to an expert in your field. For most consumers, they've never had a company add value to their lives before giving them money, only after.

Most companies are in a standoff with their potential customers. It's just like someone standing over a fire, saying, "I will give you more wood, but first, you must produce more heat!"

As the business, you must add wood (up-front value) to the fire to see a return. (new customers) There are also a couple of other benefits of creating value first and Ethical Bribes. These will enhance your chance of going on a second date and eventually closing the deal.

Becoming an Expert

Another benefit of creating Ethical Bribes is that you can paint yourself as an expert in your field. You become an expert by educating people, show that you know what you are talking about. This is important because people want to deal with experts and will pay way more for their services.

Your customers want to know that you have a complete understanding of your profession and can solve their problems with perfection. Experts can charge what they want and bring on the best clientele.

How much would you pay for life or death heart surgery? Would you rather choose a heart specialist with 30 years of experience or a general doctor that "occasionally" performs heart surgery? Who cares what the specialist charges!

I want to live!

Later on in this chapter, I will hit on the difference between benefits and features and how to create an Ethical Bribe that won't bore people to death.

Teach The Why, Sell The How

Another critical element that you can take advantage of in an Ethical Bribe is you can teach all of the reasons why your target clientele needs your services, and then sell them the solution, the how. One of the biggest problems that I see when taking on new clients is this: business owners and their employees assume that their target market knows the benefits of using their company. They skip right over the why they need it and preach the how to buy it.

Some of the most common how selling is telling people how long you have been in business, how extended your warranty is, how many employees you have, and how you are so much better than your competitor. Remember when we talked about the different levels of the brain? This is speaking directly to the neocortex.

Most of the time, your target market has no idea how much your company can help them, and even if they do, remind them every chance you get. When you talk about the why, you are communicating with the limbic part of the brain. Show that you genuinely care about them and that you just want their lives to be better. That is what business is truly all about.

When you are creating these Ethical Bribes, you must treat your audience as if it had never heard of the industry that you are in. You must tell them all of the amazing things your company does to improve their life! Remember the Key Human Driver Statement?

We already have the framework for this. All you have to do now is communicate the message to your target market. Once they understand all of the fantastic things you can do for them, then you are in the best position to sell them how to buy it.

Here's an example I implemented for one of my clients, resulting in a 440% increase in revenue for his dentistry. He wanted to bring on more clientele, and I told him I would be happy to help.

He explained that he offers free teeth cleaning because it was the best way to get people in the door. Once they were there, it was his best opportunity to sell them on the different services they provide. He was having some trouble bringing on new clients, though.

I asked him if he could choose one service to sell them, which one would it be? After a long pause, he told me that cosmetics like teeth whitening and new sets of teeth were his real money maker. I asked him what he says to them when he is trying to make a sale. He told me he hasn't really put much thought into it and usually just asks them if they want "teeth whitening." No benefits? No pre-framing? Nothing?

I asked him to gather all of the benefits of new teeth, and I would be back with a plan next week. You only need two or three key benefits.

Here were his benefits:

1. Enhances your appearance
2. Boosts self-confidence
3. Affordable

Look at what all of these benefits boiled down to, a

nice LF8 basic human desire. Can you guess which one?

When I came back, I presented my plan, and it went something like this: the first thing I would do, instead of having all of these random magazines lying around, is put out little pamphlets on the benefits of getting your teeth fixed. The TV in the waiting room should be a video or a slideshow depicting the benefits of better-looking teeth and smile!

Once he understood all of the benefits, I then showed him what to say to his target clientele to get them to want the service without being too "salesy." We also created an online marketing campaign that generated 15 new appointments in just two weeks.

Three months after he started educating people on WHY they needed fixed teeth, he saw a massive influx of people needing HOW to get it.

Benefits and Features

When you are creating these Ethical Bribes, you must remember one thing. You are only trying to hit on the emotions (benefits) of using your company. Please don't create an Ethical Bribe that is packed with logic. This is speaking on the technical aspect of things.

Benefits are how the product or service is going to make their lives better. Your potential client always purchases everything twice, once in their head, and then once from you. Remember, the potential clientele thinks in pictures and is trying to imagine in their head all of the positive emotions they will feel once they finally buy your product or service. Help them as much as you can.

Chapter Five: Your Bait

People buy with emotions and justify with logic.

Imagine that you are on the way to buy your dream car. You pull up to the dealership, and you see it sitting there. They hand you the keys, and you pull out of the dealership with a massive smile on your face. After driving around for a bit, your first stop is pulling up to your parent's house and seeing how proud they are. Next, you go to your best friend's house, and he hops in.

You step on the gas and feel the exhilaration that comes with a big engine and going fast. You're having the time of your life, and it shows!

These are all of the benefits that are flooding your brain, and I am sure you even felt a jolt of happiness while you imagined it. The features are going to be what confirms that you made the right decision. Things like the warranty or the dependability that a new car brings, that's your logic.

Car companies like Mercedes-Benz understand this point very well and have profited off it for years. The commercials typically include a very good looking male or female and imply that you get this car, you will simply be better than everyone and get the companion of your dreams. Every commercial they make communicates directly to one of the key human drivers.

Before we break into the actual creation of your Ethical Bribe, go back and review your Key Human Driver Statement and make sure that you have a complete understanding of what your selling point is.

For example, if your company's basic human desire is about survival, enjoyment of life, and life extension, make sure that your Ethical Bribe and the headline hint at how you will help them achieve this desire.

This is why it's so essential to establish a solid foundation first. If you are unsure who your target market is and what is truly important to them, you will never create an Ethical Bribe that will convert. There are different forms of Ethical Bribes that you can use.

Below are the most common types of Ethical Bribes I have found from The Conversion Code by Chris Smith:

1. Guide/Report/eBook: when you build a guide, report, or eBook, you are able to give your potential clients more perceived value. For example, when I take the time to create *Free Guide On How to Influence Your Target Market on a Subconscious Level,* it increases conversions massively compared to a blog post!

2. Cheat Sheets/Checklists: quick wins, short cuts, these are things that people just gravitate to. *Cheat Sheet: How To Grow Your Company With Facebook Marketing.*
3. Toolkit/Resource list: this is where the *Top 10 Best Apps to have to Ensure Your Family's Safety this Summer* comes into play. Helpful content that is quick and easy to deliver.
4. Webinar: a webinar is basically an online class or discussion. People register for a spot and you teach them through video.
5. Free Trial: Free one month trial of your products or services. This is very common for software.
6. Quiz or survey: By far this is one of my favorite ethical bribe tools to use. Create a quiz on if someone is right for your company. Try websites like TryInteract.com or Playbuzz. com.

Creating The Headline

Now that you have a solid Ethical Bribe, you need to structure your headline so that everyone in your target market will be interested, not just the people already in the market to buy.

Chet Holmes explains it the best in his book, The Ultimate Sales Machine, like this;

"About 3% of potential buyers at any given time are buying now. Right now. That percentage drives all commerce. My research further concludes that 7% of the population is open to the idea of buying. This is the percentage who may be dissatisfied with their current provider, but not necessarily buying now. The remaining 90% fall into one of three equal categories. The top third is what we call 'not thinking about it.' They are not against it, not for it, but just "not thinking about it."

"The next third is what we call 'think they are not interested.' So at first pass, they are not neutral like the first third. They would reply, 'I don't think we are interested right now.'

"The final third is what I call 'definitely not interested.' They are happy with what they have or simply know they just do not need it!"

How can you create a headline that grabs the attention of all of your target market and not just the top 10%? Make it broad enough to apply to everyone in the market, not only the people who are ready to buy. Here's a tip that I've learned that helps me create the best headlines without excluding 90% of my target market. Focus on the key benefit that you are bringing to them and work from there. Grab your Key Human Driver Statement and work from there.

Here's a list of headlines that you can use to infuse your Ethical Bribe into:

Opening with a Question

- Are you curious about...?
- Have you ever stayed up at night thinking about...?
- Do you ever ask yourself...?
- Are you secretly afraid of...?
- Looking for just the right...?
- Tired of empty promises from...?
- Tired of the same old...?

Opening with a Statement

- Let me ask you a simple question.
- We will change your mind about...
- It's not every day that...
- Here's an idea worth considering.
- Don't let ___ keep you from getting ahead.
- Don't be caught without ___.
- ___ often spells the difference between failure and success.
- If you are like most people, you probably...

- We live in an increasingly complex world.
- Today, more than ever...
- It's never too late to...
- Let's talk about why you need ___.
- Let's face it.
- Let's be honest.

Don't have a headline that states, "The Top 5 Reasons You Need A New Furnace." Instead, say, "The Top 5 Ways Homeowners Can Save Up To 50% On Their Electric Bill This Winter!" Do you see the difference? Everyone on earth wants to save money. Once they understand that your furnace may be what drives up their electric bill, they will be more inclined to buy! You're Teaching the Why, Selling the How.

Don't have a headline that states, "The Top 5 Reasons To Get Your Teeth Whitened." Instead, say, "The Single Most Important Thing To Do If You Want To Get Ahead In Life!" Within the Ethical Bribe, you will explain that the first thing people do when meeting you for the first time is to look at your teeth. You'll also explain the benefits that come with being more self-confident. Everyone wants to get ahead in life, simple as that. Once they understand something as simple as what teeth whitening can do for them, they will be more likely to convert and turn into a client.

Don't have a headline that states, "The Most Effective Workouts for Mothers!" Instead, say, "The Top 5 Ways Mothers Can Have More Energy and Feel Great!" Again, within the Ethical Bribe, it can boil down to workouts. The key is not scaring them away too early.

Most people have no idea what the true benefits of your company, products, or services are. When you're creating your headline, you just want to pique their interest just enough that they want to know more and click to get the Ethical Bribe. They learn the tremendous benefits of what your company provides, and now you have a greater chance of converting them into a customer.

Let's say your headline is, "The Best Way To Live A Longer, Healthier, and Happier Life." Your Ethical Bribe content might truly be the five reasons to buy a bike, and that's fine. Also, throw in different food options, how to sleep better at night, and general tips that will help them live a better life. You just have to ensure that the Ethical Bribe's content explains how biking will enable you to live a longer, healthier, and happier life.

Let's look at an example of a headline that I might use for my imaginary business, Bikes & Stuff. "The Five Reasons to Ride A Bike!" The people that aren't in the market for a bike would skip right over this. Instead, say "Cheat Sheet: The Best Way To Live A Longer, Healthier and Happier Life!" Do you want to live a longer, healthier, and happier life? Of course, you do.

Within the actual content they download, I'll explain how biking will enable them to live longer, healthier, and happier lives. I will also throw in tips about the best foods to eat, supplements to take, meditation, and stretching exercises. Now they are picturing themselves on a bike and feeling all of the emotions associated with living a longer, healthier, and happier life. Always start by creating the entire Ethical Bribe first, then make the headline. It will be way easier in the long run.

Bonus: Conversion Rate Down? Use Mystery

Why is Leonardo da Vinci's Mona Lisa considered one of the most famous paintings of all time? She is mysterious! Is she smiling? If so, what is she smiling about?

Create an Ethical Bribe that solves a mystery. The human brain needs closure and will do whatever possible to get it.

One of my favorite ways to increase the conversion rate for downloads of my Ethical Bribe is using mystery.

A couple of years ago, I was having a terribly hard time getting conversions for one of my clients. After pulling an all-nighter the night before preparing for the meeting, I stumbled across what we needed to do, which was to use mystery.

Instead of going home the night before the meeting, I decided to stay at my office because I knew I would not get a single minute of shuteye. After discovering what we needed to do going forward though, I slipped off my shoes and leaned back in my chair to try and get one or two hours of sleep. Around 3:30 am, I heard a loud bang from the office kitchen; it sounded like someone has climbed the fire escape and had broken the window.

I opened my office door to investigate what was going on, assuming that it was just the janitor knocking over a glass. To my complete shock and horror, once I saw who it was, I knew I had to get out of there fast.

When I arrived at her office in the heart of downtown, I entered the elevator and clicked the 42nd floor. I was so excited to show her the plan I had created and knew that our drought for leads and interactions was over. After I proposed my plan, she agreed and loved it. I told her we needed to create a 30-second video advertisement posing the mystery and making people go to the landing page to download the Ethical Bribe to get closure.

Two years later, this client's campaign is still running and produces outstanding results for her company to this day.

If you are like most people, your brain was a bit upset when I didn't tell you who was in my kitchen. You probably felt a little annoyed that I didn't tell you right then and there. This is the part of the advertisement that would ask you to click on the link for the rest of the story.

Remember, you do not have to use fear or scare tactics

in your mystery campaign. Any key human drivers can use this method; all you have to do is understand where to leave the cliff hanger and tell them where to get closure. Try this method out for at least one of your Ethical Bribes.

As for my story? Well, that day we had hung up new curtains in our kitchen. When the air conditioning turned on, it made the curtains blow, and it knocked over a glass. When I opened my door, it looked like a ghost, and I got scared. I truly felt like my life was in danger.

SECRETS RECAP:

Make sure that you take the time to create an Ethical Bribe that your target clientele will want to download so you can get their information.

1. Create an amazing headline that will grab the attention of every person in your target market.
2. Make sure the content that your target market downloads are packed with quality information.
3. Think long term and create a fantastic Ethical Bribe!

Ethical Bribe

_____

_____

_____

_____

Chapter Five: Your Bait

_____
_____
_____
_____
_____

Headline For Ethical Bribe:

_____
_____
_____
_____
_____
_____
_____
_____

CHAPTER SIX: CREATING THE ADVERTISEMENTS

In this chapter, we will cover:

- Which avenues to focus on based on your target market profile
- How to insert your Ethical Bribe into each platform
- Split Test Bracketing
- Stair Step Budgeting

So far, we have established The Foundation and created an amazing Ethical Bribe to persuade our Target Market to give us their contact information. The next step we are going to tackle is to create the advertisements. Before you launch the campaign, make sure that you read Chapter Seven. All of the campaigns we will be making will have a pause button or will allow you to save it as a draft. Create the outline, but wait to go live until you read the next chapter.

The focus of this chapter is going to be showing you the best way to insert your Ethical Bribe into the different avenues of digital marketing. Creating the ads is the easy part of this whole process. The part that most companies struggle with is understanding how to create a message that will generate conversions.

Avenues To Use

In Chapter Three, we took some time and developed your company's Target Market Profile. This is when you will need to pull it back out and assess which avenues will best reach your target market.

The two main categories of online marketing are:

- Social Media Marketing (Facebook, Instagram, LinkedIn, Ect.)
- Search Engine Marketing (Google, Bing)

Pro Tip:

Once you assess all of the options in this chapter, dedicate yourself to two or three and master them.

Facebook

Ahh, the good old Zucc machine. You can never go wrong with Facebook when marketing your company. I know that in recent times they have been under constant scrutiny but ignore it. Despite the large number of people saying they will "delete their Facebook profile," it saw a massive increase in new profile creations in 2019.

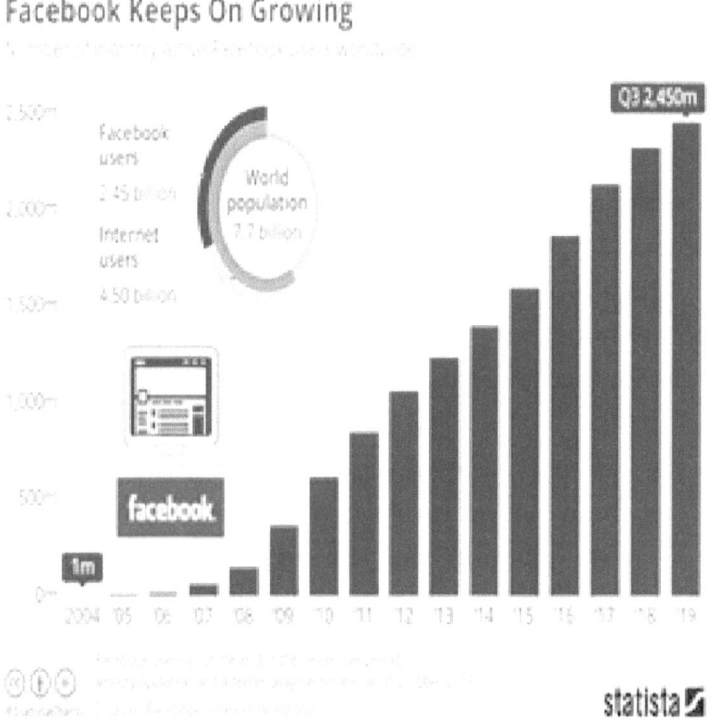

I hear some of you already complaining about how Facebook marketing hasn't worked for you and how it is a waste of money, but I have a little secret I want to let you in on. It wasn't Facebook that got you the poor results; it was your message and the desired outcome you were trying to achieve.

Facebook marketing is a vital aspect of growing your business because you are getting introduced to new people within your target market. The key with Facebook is NOT to try and sell from the advertisement, but to get people to act on your Ethical Bribe!

Why shouldn't you try to sell on Facebook? In general, Facebook and social media are places where people go to get away from it all, an escape from reality. This is most people's "safe zone," and if you try to pitch them during this time, you will be disregarded and ignored. That is why you see so many people frustrated with Facebook marketing. They simply don't understand this essential piece of the puzzle.

Make sure that when you are creating a Facebook ad, you are not coming off aggressive. We are merely offering a way for them to achieve:

1. Survival, enjoyment of life, life extension
2. Enjoyment of food and beverages
3. Freedom from fear, pain, and danger
4. Sexual companionship
5. Comfortable living conditions
6. To be superior, winning, keeping up with the Joneses
7. Care and protection of loved ones
8. Social approval

Once they truly feel like you are just trying to make their lives better, that is when you will see some real traction. Later on, in this book, I will teach you how to convert these leads in to some of your best, most loyal clientele. For now, you are just trying to help them out. This is asking them for their number to get a second, third, and fourth date.

Chapter Six: Creating The Advertisements

Facebook usage among key demographics.

Simply put, your Target Market is on Facebook, and you need to allocate some of your advertising dollars to this avenue.

Setting Up Your Facebook Campaign

Being able to understand the best way to insert your Ethical Bribe into a Facebook advertisement is critical for your success. Facebook has made it extremely easy to set up the backend work of creating your campaign. Make sure you are referencing your Target Market Profile Sheet when creating the demographics of your advertisement.

To start, I want you to pull out your sheet with your:

- Target Market Profile
- Key Human Driver Statement
- Ethical Bribe
- Headline For Ethical Bribe

Target Market Profile

Make sure when you are targeting the right demographic when you are setting up your advertisement.

Key Human Driver Statement

Our Key Human Driver Statement is there for reference, so after we create the advertisement, we can make sure we are communicating with our key human driver. Ask yourself, "Does this hit on my KHD statement or not?"

Ethical Bribe

Have you created your Ethical Bribe? Make sure the content is done and ready to send before launching the advertisement. We'll also be using the headline in all of our ads, and I find it pleasant to just have it right in front of me.

Facebook has three sections that we need to fill out.

1. Headline
2. Description

Photo or video

For the headline, use the headline that you created for your Ethical Bribe. Let's say I was a proud owner of a bike shop called Bikes and Stuff. For our headline, it would be "The Best Way To Live A Longer, Healthier, and Happier Life."

For the description, we will elaborate on our headline and sell our Ethical Bribe. The trick here is to give them just enough for them to want to know more. Remember the mystery section earlier in the book? This works very well for Facebook marketing. You want them to get fear of missing out from your description.

The Photo or Video is the part where almost all of my clients have trouble. If possible, always go with a video. If you are the type of person that can get in front of a camera and preach, do it! The best return I have ever received from an advertisement was when I had the actual Ethical Bribe in my hand and talked about the benefits it would bring to them.

It sounded like this:

"Hi, my name is Cooper Saunders, and what I have here in my hand will change your business forever. I have thrown together the most valuable cheat sheet to ensure you dominate your competitors by using the same strategy that all the most successful organizations have used from Alexander the Great, all the way down to Steve Jobs and Jeff Bezos.

Do you want to make more money, all while cutting expenses? Have you identified your Grand Strategy for your business and then established tactical steps to ensure you get there? Click the link down below, and I will personally send this to you now!"

Short and to the point. There are a lot of questions that I left open that they will want the answer to.

- "What is a Grand Strategy?"
- "Damn, Big claim. Alexander The Great, Steve Jobs, and Jeff Bezos?"
- "Yes, I want to make money and cut expenses. How?"
- "Dominate my competitors while spending less money? Might be worth the click..."
- "Am I moving toward my goals?"

I'm not trying to get them to hand over their card information, just their contact information. If you're not comfortable with talking in front of the camera, try and hire someone. If you have a Facebook ad with just a photo, you're drastically bringing down the conversion rate by at least 50 percent.

There are also awesome websites where you can create template videos. They're not the best for conversions, but better than photos. If you hop on Google and search "template video maker," you will get a handful, and they are all good.

Now, Facebook is also very special because you can

capture a lead without making them leave the platform. When you log in to the ads manager and click "create a new campaign," there will be an option for a lead generation campaign.

This is massive. You want your Target Market to be able to get your Ethical Bribe in the quickest and easiest way possible.

Now that you understand the basics of creating your Facebook Marketing campaign, you will have a new love for this gold mine called Facebook!

At the end of the chapter, I will hit on a couple of tips and tricks that will help you get better results for all of your marketing campaigns, but for now, we will move on to the second avenue of Social Media Marketing.

Instagram Ads

Instagram is owned and operated by Facebook, so the strategy remains the same. The only difference between Facebook and Instagram is the age difference. Instagram tends to have a bit of a younger audience, so if that fits your target market, this might be for you!

YouTube

Owned by Google, YouTube is another place people go to relax and get away from it all. Keep your message short and sweet like Facebook, and you will be just fine! Some people might argue that YouTube is a search engine, and I would have to agree to an extent. In my opinion, YouTube has set up their ads to feel more like social media.

2019 YouTube Age Demographics

- Over 90% of 18-44-year-old American internet users watch videos on YouTube.
- Over 80% of 45-64-year-old American internet users watch videos on YouTube.
- Over half of American internet users who are aged 65 and over, watch videos on YouTube.
- 59% of Generation Z (16-24-year-olds) have increased their YouTube usage since last year.
- 46% of millennials (25-34-year-olds) have increased their YouTube usage since last year.
- 70% of millennial YouTube users watched a YouTube video to learn how to do something new or learn about something they're interested in.

Source Hubspot.com

You can see that YouTube has a very wide array of users, and I can almost guarantee that your target market is on there watching videos. This is another platform that is not lacking traffic; the hard part is creating a message that will get our target market's attention and generate conversions.

We will turn your Ethical Bribe into a 30-second long video, with the first 5-15 seconds being the headline of your Ethical Bribe. This is the headline method I call

"Punch In The Face." Why? Because it is so surprising and draws massive attention from your target clientele.

The most time you will have to grab the attention of your prospect is around three-toseven seconds. You want to wake your target market up and pop them in the face with your enthusiasm and passion. Grab their attention! Like Mike Tyson once said, "Everyone has a plan until they get punched in the face." That's what your headline should do, a virtual punch in the face! They planned to watch a YouTube video, but now they are downloading your Ethical Bribe!

If you do not want to be on camera, this might not be the route for you, but remember, people love authenticity. When they see someone that genuinely cares about helping them succeed in life, you will see a massive conversion rate. Don't worry about it being professional. Most smartphones these days will do the trick! You're simply trying to give them information that will help them live a better life. Not selling or being too aggressive.

I like to think about generating leads from Facebook, Instagram, and YouTube like you are trying to get your desired partner to take an interest in you. Just offering yourself, and if they like what they can see, they can hop on the train. If not, it's their loss. Make sure you are giving this vibe from your advertisements.

Another great thing about YouTube advertising is that you can collect the leads from the platform, just like Facebook. The more comfortable you can make it for the prospect to give you their information, the better.

Another thing that you might want to consider with YouTube is The Power of Association.

In Robert Cialdini's bestselling book, PreSuasion, he hits on the power of associations. "At the start of the callers' work shifts, all were given information to help them communicate the value of contributing to the cause for which they were soliciting (a local university). Some of the callers got the information printed on plain paper. Other callers got the identical information carrying a photo of a runner winning a race. It was a photo that had previously shown to stir achievementrelated thinking. Remarkably, by the end of their three-hour shifts, the second sample callers had raised 60 percent more money than their comparable coworkers."

The power of association is real, and you must do everything in your power to be associated with the message you are trying to communicate. With YouTube, when your advertisement is played before "Charlie Bit My Finger," your company will be associated with what the watcher feels from that video. If it's happiness, you will be associated with happiness and vice versa. This will most likely happen on a subconscious level, which is even more powerful.

Suppose the main benefit of your Ethical Bribe is health; set up your advertisements to play in front of videos about well-being and happiness. If you Ethical Bribe's main benefit is family safety, play your advertisement in front of something parents or families would watch.

The power of association is not only for YouTube but for every marketing platform. Sometimes you might not have complete control over it but do everything in your power to make sure your brand is associated with your main benefit. Play happy music in your video's background and use colors that signify your desired emotion you want them to feel.

LinkedIn

LinkedIn was created to make connections in your professional life. When I first joined LinkedIn, I made the awful mistake to mark myself as a "business owner," and long story short, I would get around 20 direct message advertisements a day.

You would think that people on LinkedIn might be a little better with creating messages, being professionals and all, but nope. It is the exact same experience.

Puking information on me, telling me how great their product is, and only speaking to my Neocortex. Not only that, but most of them assumed that I needed to reach out to them, like this one below.

Here is an example of what the typical message looks like:

Hey Cooper,

"I'm the CEO at _____, located right outside of Philadelphia (we're a commercial lending broker). We offer Term Loans, Lines of Credit, Invoice Factoring, PO Financing, Equipment Leasing, and Working Capital Advances. I work with business owners who have a tendency to tell me one of three things...

They do not have enough funding from an existing bank line to continue growing their business at this rate.
They're stressed waiting on their A/R from progressive or milestone billing.

They feel pressured to meet deadlines or pay contractors upfront and need funding quickly to keep the business moving.

If any of that's relevant and worth a conversation, I'd love to hear from you. Submit the form and I will provide all the information you need. If right now is not the right time that is ok too, just keep me in mind for future consideration."

To start, I don't care if you are the CEO or where you are located. Next, rather than telling me the benefit of the services he provides, he hits me with, "we're a commercial lending broker." Right there, he knocked out 90 percent of his leads.

Could he be any more depressing on the reasons business owners contact him? Rather than telling me all of the shitty situations your clientele have been in, flip it so that you are explaining how happy they were once you did your job! Paint the picture inside my brain of how much better my life will be once I do business with you.

Cardinal Rule #1 broken all over the place. Can you spot where? All he is talking about are the features of what he does, and has not touched on benefits, not once!

Now, after this massive waste of time, he then moves onto this line, "If any of that's relevant and worth a conversation, I'd love to hear from you." Psssh, I'm sure you would.

There was nothing there that spoke to my Key Human Drivers or offered anything of value. You can also guarantee this guy got a solid zero percent conversion rate and went on to tell all of his buddies how marketing doesn't work and it is a waste of time.

If you are business to business, it is massively important to make sure you give before you receive. Add wood before you expect to get heat. Use your Key Human Driver statement, create an Ethical Bribe, and for the love of God, do not do this. It always boils down to the message, not the platform.

Social media marketing is all about creating that first interaction with the potential customer. You must remember that you are interrupting something that they are doing, and if you don't come with anything that will stop and catch their attention, you will be throwing money out the window.

For Social Media Marketing, it is the same strategy no matter which platform you decide to use. Offer value, get their contact information and close later.

Search Engine Marketing

SEM or Search Engine Marketing is a little different than social media marketing. Instead of introducing yourself to the target audience, you are getting placed in front of people searching for something based on the keywords they use. Don't overthink it. Just stick to the basics.

When you search on Google, what do you see? A bunch of advertisements that focus on the features of their business, the how. That won't be us. We're different.

We're better. When we search on Google, 90 percent of the time, it is just information gathering. We are just trying to learn more about a product or service. When creating our headline, our job is to catch all of these "drifters" so that we are the first choice when they make a decision.

Your headline is going to be the same, but with one modification. Let's say that people are searching for "best bikes" or "bikes near me." In our headline, we can put "The Six Ways to Live a Longer, Happier, and Healthier Life on a Bike." You don't need to introduce the idea to people that are already searching for a bike; they know they want a bike, now you just have to paint yourself as the expert and hit the emotional buttons!

Imagine that you are in the market for a bike, you go on Google and search "Bikes for sale," and you have the option between these three headlines, which one are you most likely to choose?

1. "Buy Your New Bike Here. BikeSellers Direct"
2. "Cheap Bikes For You! Free Shipping!"
3. "Bikes For Sale! The Six Ways to Live a Longer, Happier, and Healthier Life on a Bike."

The last choice is a breath of fresh air, and almost had me convinced that I need a bike, and I wrote it myself! What are the underlying benefits of your product or service? You should already have this created, right?

REMEMBER:

- Emotions over logic
- Benefit over features
- Explain the why, sell the how

Always understand that no matter where you are marketing, the results come from understanding human tendencies and how to influence their decisions.

Now that you understand SEM and SMM's tactics and how to create an amazing message, you need to set up the campaign correctly on the backend. You can have the best message and the best Ethical Bribe, but if you do not reach the right people, you will lose before getting started.

If you are not 100% sure about setting up and launching the campaign, hire an expert, or watch online tutorials on how to do it. Since you have all of the content, you can most likely get a pretty good deal from a digital marketing company. Just make sure you are using an established company that knows what they are doing.

Budget

Start small, and increase the amount of money in the ads that are working. Simple as that. Every single advertisement that you make needs to have an A/B split test. The A/B split test is creating the same advertisement but with different content.

You might have a video in advertisement A and a photo in advertisement B. You are testing the waters to see what works and what does not.

To start any campaign, this is what I do, and it has always produced excellent advertisements.

The first thing I do is create at least ten different variations of the same advertisement. After that, I set them up in brackets just like they do in tournaments like March Madness. I launch all ten of them with a budget of something small, like $3/day.

After a couple of days, I check on the advertisements and see which ones performed better than their counterparts. Whichever advertisement did better got to move up the bracket, and the one who lost gets thrown out. Eventually, it makes it up to the finals, and whichever advertisement won gets to run for about a month or so, then I do it all over again.

There are a couple of different ways to measure the performance of an advertisement. It could be on the click-through rate, clicks to your landing page, or leads generated.

All of the other metrics, like impressions, are a waste of time. Depending on how intense you are, you can make a bigger bracket and test as many advertisements as you want. The most I have seen was right around 100 or so, which was insane, but they produced one of the best performing advertisements I have seen to date. The advertisement produces 20-30 leads a day, while the company spends less than 20 cents per lead.

The more testing that you do, the better your advertisements will be. How different would your company be if you were bringing on 20-30 new leads a day?

Another big factor that you must consider is that marketing is an investment, and the more money you put

Chapter Six: Creating The Advertisements

in, the more you will get out. That being said, marketing is not gambling. Before you go all in, make sure that you see stable returns. Stairstep your way to success. If you see an advertisement that is working, throw more money at it. If you see an advertisement that has poor returns, shut it down.

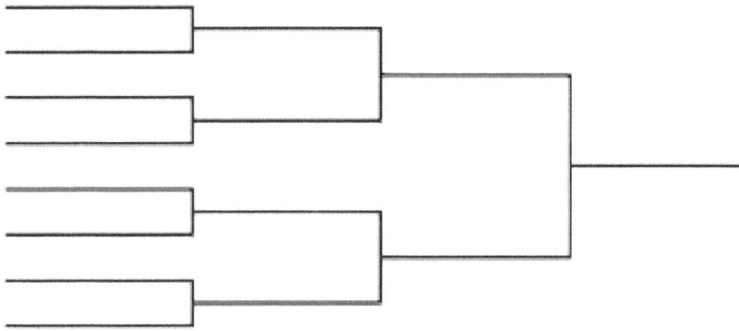

If you're hiring a marketing company, make sure you get an itemized list of how much money is going to the advertisements and how much is going to the agency. Make sure you take the time to spit test your advertisements and stair-step your way to success.

SECRETS RECAP:

Social media platforms such as Facebook, YouTube, and Instagram are places where people go to socialize. They go to see pictures of their kids or grandkids, watch funny videos.
They use it as a place to relax. Ensure you understand this and frame your message so that it doesn't feel like you are selling them, just trying to make their lives better.

These types of advertisements are introducing you to your target clientele for the first time, and you know what they say about first impressions. Capture the leads, and then close them later.

Search engine marketing such as Google Search Advertising is a bit different in that the potential clients are actively looking for a product or service.

Don't overthink it, and remember the basics. Focus on how you will make their lives better and speak to their Key Human Driver. After you have set up the ads, make sure you split test at least ten of them to ensure that the ad you eventually go with is the best option. Once the best version of the advertisement is identified, stair-step the ad spend. The more you make from the ad, the more money you will put into the advertisement.

Now that we are getting traffic, we need to understand the best way to capture all of these leads.

CHAPTER SEVEN: CAPTURE THE LEAD

Now that you have set up your foundation correctly, and the ads are created and set to launch, you need to ensure that you send all of your traffic to a well-constructed landing page. A landing page is a stand-alone page separate from your site, with the sole intention of generating conversions.

Why Don't I Just Send People To My Main Site?

On average, humans have an attention span of less than eight seconds. For context, goldfish have better attention spans than we do at nine seconds. That's why you must guide your target market along the Yellow Brick Road and make it very easy to find your Ethical Bribe. When you send them to your company's main site, they will get confused and leave.

Back in 2003, Microsoft came across a problem. Conversion rates for online sales were insufficient for their flagship business product, Office. The IT team at Microsoft decided to try out a radical idea, create a website for the sole intention of generating conversion, nothing else.

Here is how Wikipedia defines a landing page:

"Landing pages are often linked to social media, email campaigns, or search engine marketing campaigns to enhance the advertisements' effectiveness. The general goal of a landing page is to convert site visitors into sales or leads. If the goal is to obtain a lead, the landing page will include some method for the visitor to get into contact with the company, usually a phone number, or an inquiry form. If a sale is required, the landing page will usually have a link for the visitor to click, which will then send them to a shopping cart or a checkout area. By analyzing activity generated by the linked URL, marketers can use click-through rates and conversion rate to determine the success of an advertisement."

Our landing page's job is to convert traffic from advertisements into leads to start the process of turning the lead into a loyal customer. Let's break down the steps to create a landing page that will generate conversions for your business. Remember, Keep It Simple, Silly. As Chris Smith said in his book, The Conversion Code, "Because human brains process visuals 60,000 times faster than they do text, a critical component of cracking the conversion code is understanding that a key aspect is design, not words, builds trust online." Here's a blog post from Kissmetrics entitled, Anatomy of a Perfect Landing Page. Here are the top seven that they suggested. I also added my take on each essential element.

Your Headline

The headline needs to have the same message as the headline of the advertisement that you created. For the most part, you want your landing page to look identical to your advertisement: same colors, same video, same feel. Most likely, it will be the Ethical Bribe headline, so you need to make sure these add up. Don't try and be fancy with this. Be concise and straightforward.

Subheading

The subheading will break off from the headline and hit on a key benefit that the visitor will receive from the information. If your Ethical Bribe headline was "Cheat Sheet: The Best Way To Live A Longer, Healthier and Happier Life!" your subheading will want to say something like, "Tired of the same old boring routine? Learn the tips and tricks to turn your life around for the better!" You're just elaborating and reinforcing the key reason they clicked on the Ethical Bribe in the first place, to live a longer, healthier, and happier life.

Description

The most effective description ot he key benefits they will receive from this download in bullet point form. Make sure that your landing page is pointing ot he desired outcome, downloading the Ethical Bribe. Keep it short and sweet.

Testimonials

The testimonial isn't about how great your company is. It's about how much your Ethical Bribe helped them. The testimonial is telling the visitor that they need this content before it's too late.

Call To Action

Make sure the focal point of your landing page is the form to download the Ethical Bribe. Don't make it hard to find.

Keep the form to, at most, three entries:

1. Name
2. Number
3. Email

Ensure that the person who is putting in the email knows how they will receive the content. We do this to make sure that they do not give us a fake email address. Some people are weird about giving out their phone number, so you can make that optional if you want. At the bottom of the form, include the button with "Get Now" or "Download Now."

Remove Links

We don't want them to be able to navigate wherever they want to go. Please don't give them the option to click on the menu and learn about your company. The only thing that should be in the header is your logo; that's it.

Optimize For Mobile

More than half of the traffic that will come to the site will be on mobile, so make sure that it looks great here too. The only thing you truly want on the mobile view is the headline, the secondary headline, and the form. Some of my favorite software that you can create landing pages from templates are Clickfunnels.com or leadpages.com. You can also create lead pages from traditional website builders like Wix, WordPress, or GoDaddy. Just make sure that you follow the steps above.

As for your domain, my recommendation is to buy a new one that you will use for all of your Ethical Bribes and offers. If possible, make sure that your name is in the domain. With my company WiseGuys, our landing page domains look like this.

- WiseGuysOffer.com
- WiseGuysLearn.com
- WiseGuysdm.net
- WiseGuysEducate.com

Make sure that your name is somewhere in the domain. A few years ago, I had a client complaining that he was not getting any conversions on his landing page. I was confused because I had set up his landing page and was very proud of my work. The only thing I didn't watch over was which domain he chose.

My client was in the legal profession and offered a free quiz to see if a divorce was right for his target prospect. It was one of the better Ethical Bribes I have seen, so again, I knew it wasn't that. Then I asked him what domain he went with for his landing page. Then, after a long pause, he told his domain name, "ProstheticLegs.net."

After a moment of silence, I asked him why in the world he would choose that domain? He then proceeded to tell me that he wanted to save some money, so he called around to some of his buddies to see if they had a domain that they don't use anymore, and his buddy gave him this! Not only that, he decided to use it!

I couldn't help but laugh. Domains are not expensive. I suggested that we buy the domain ShouldIGetDivorced.net and even bought it for him, a massive $11.99 purchase.

After we fixed the domain, his quiz was generated 2-5 leads a day, and he has been massively busy ever since. Remember, don't try and save money on things that will produce tremendous results in the future. If not, it will come back to but you in the butt, or the prosthetic leg.

Aesthetically Pleasing

Now that you have the foundation of what the landing page outline will look like and the best way to choose a domain is, it's time to make sure your landing page is aesthetically pleasing. If you're not particularly tech-savvy, we have a list of the top website creators that we can recommend that we have tested and prescreened. For more information, visit our site WiseGuysDM.com.

The first thing that you must do is make sure your site has a clean feel to it. Don't make the background of your landing page orange or add a massively big or unique image. You want to keep the background look simple so that the actual content you add to the site will pop. My rule of thumb is to keep the background white on your landing pages.

All of the images that you add should be crisp and the right size. There's nothing worse than going to a website and all of their images are blurry. If you don't have professional photos of your own, there are plenty of sites that you can get images from. Here are a few of my favorites:

- Pixabay.com
- Pexels.com
- Unsplash.com

Another thing, please make sure that the font you are using is simple and elegant. Most of the time, when you are creating a landing page, the default font will be just fine. I know that this is a given to most of you, but I've had a couple of clients who have used interesting fonts, like Comic Sans.

Pleasing Big Tech

Not only do you need to please the traffic you are sending to your landing page, but also the Google and Facebook editor that will be reviewing it. If they deem your landing page unacceptable, they will disapprove your advertisement and even suspend or ban your account.

Here are the five main items that Google believes makes a good landing page to ensure optimal "User Experience."

In Perry Marshall's book, The Ultimate Guide To Google Adwords, he breaks down the five key components.

1. Relevant, useful, and original content. Your page's copy and images must maintain the scent and clearly relate to your ad text and keyword.
2. Transparency and trustworthiness. Be open and transparent about your business and its products and services. Be transparent with visitors (on your page or via a link) what you plan to do with the personal information they share with you.
3. Easy navigation. The simpler, the better. When your visitor can easily find on the page what you promised in the ad, she'll stick around and take action.
4. Fast-Loading pages. Pages that load slowly fare poorly with your visitors and with Google, too.

PageSpeed Insights is a terrific tool you can use to check your page's loading time. Just search for the "Google Page Speed Insight" in the search bar, and it will pull right up.
5. Mobile-friendliness. Now, more than 50 percent of traffic comes from mobile devices. You're better off designing your landing pages for mobile-first and then polishing them off for tablet or desktop viewing.

Most people just focus on the best ways to convert traffic into leads but forget that they must also please the reviewers at Google and Facebook. Take the time and make sure that your landing page falls within the guidelines above.

Split Test

Remember in the previous chapter when I hit on making sure you split test your advertisements? This is the same concept, but there are many more things that you will be able to change and edit on a landing page. Set up two or three and test them against each other once you have found the best advertisement to go with. It's a lot of work, but it could mean the difference between a six-figure and a seven-figure year for your business.

Close 'em Now?

Now that we understand the basics of what makes a good landing page, I want to talk about closing them after collecting the customer's information. Most of the people that have requested your Ethical Bribe will want to read it. You'll have to follow up with email or text message marketing and eventually close them that way, and that's fine. Most people do not want to get married on the first date, but some will, and you need to make sure that you at least offer them the option!

After they request your information, you will have a confirmation page. Most companies have something that says, "Thank you for submitting your information. Please let us know if it does not reach you!" Nothing special, but it does the job. What if we could use this message to increase the likelihood that this prospect will turn into a client? What if you could upsell the client with this message? The hardest part of this whole process is getting the first interaction with the client. All the rest of the steps will be easy, and once you get that initial interaction, that's when the real fun begins.

When I went in to buy my new computer, it took me MONTHS to build up the courage to go to the Apple Store and buy my Mac. Once I was there, I found myself getting all of the features, storage, and every single "dongle" I laid my eyes upon.

Depending on which industry you are in, this step could go one of two ways:

1. Try and sell the customer a product
2. Try and schedule an appointment, or call.

Let's look at my bike shop, Bikes & Stuff. For me, I could go one of two ways. I could try and sell them on a new bike from my eCommerce store or get them to schedule an appointment to come to my shop. If you are a service-based business and cannot sell your products over the internet, try and have them schedule a call or an appointment. It helps if you include some kind of offer or incentive for them to take action.

This step aims to give the people that are ready to go now an option to do so. Suppose they aren't, no worries. We'll contact them after they read the Ethical Bribe and understand how much our services can help them. These people simply don't want to get married on the first date, and I don't blame them.

Another technique you can use is offering another Ethical Bribe after having already downloaded the first one. You would want to do this so that you can separate the interested from the ultra-interested leads. If they request more than one article from you, it's imperative that they get treated differently.

For these ultra-interested leads, you need to craft a specific follow up procedure for them. For the leads that fall into the WiseGuys UltraInterested Category, I give them a call personally. I ask if they had any questions about the content and try to close them on a service we provide. The choice is yours. What technique are you going to use on your confirmation page to increase the rate of clients using your business?

1. Upsell them with a product (eCommerce)
2. Schedule an appointment (SBB, B2B)
3. Another Ethical Bribe (Ultra-Interested)

Remember to always get their contact information first.

Delivering The Ethical Bribe

So, the potential client has requested the Ethical Bribe; what now? You need to make sure that as soon as they request it, you send it. The longer they wait for the information, the less interested they are.

Depending on the website creator you are using, it should have a couple of options available for you. Website creators like WordPress or ClickFunnels have plugins that you can use, so you do not alienate your potential clients with a false delivery.

SECRETS RECAP:

- Create a landing page that is designed to turn traffic into a conversion - Split Test Your Landing Pages - Close 'em now?
- Deliver with automation software

CHAPTER EIGHT: CONVERSIONS

"*Ladies and Gentlemen, welcome to the main event...*" This is the main event, The Evander Holyfield Vs. Mike Tyson, Muhammad Ali Vs. Joe Frazer. This is when we turn leads into paying customers. All of the work that we have done so far has led us to this moment; now, it is time to reap the rewards for all of our hard work. In this chapter, we will walk through the exact steps you will need to take to nurture and eventually convert your leads into paying customers.

The first step that we must take in the conversion process is to nurture the prospect and continuously provide them with substantial value. It takes around 8-12 follow-ups and interactions for a lead to turn into a paying customer. Simply put, the money is in the follow-up.

How many times on average do you think the typical business follows up with a lead before giving up? By the fourth contact, 89.8% of businesses have given up. We're going to be different.

THE LIFECYCLE OF TURNING LEADS INTO
PAYING CUSTOMERS

CONTACT #1
50% of companies have given up on the lead.

CONTACT #2
65% of companies have given up on the lead.

CONTACT #3
80% of companies have given up on the lead.

CONTACT #4
92% of companies have given up on the lead.

CONTACT #5
The lead starts to get familiar with your company.

CONTACT #6
The lead slowly gets more and more comfortable with your brand.

CONTACT #7
You are starting to transition from stranger, and earn top of mind awareness.

CONTACT #8
Your target prospect is starting to think they should give your business a chance.

CONTACT #9
Your prospect has started preparing to give your business a call.

CONTACT #10
Familiar household name with prospect.

CONTACT #11
Prospect has used your company and is now referring you to their friends and family.

CONTACT #12
The lead has turned into an evangelist, and is a walking advertisement for your company!

The Basics of Conversions

Before we even think about asking the prospect to use our company, we need to nurture the relationship. We need them to get to know us more, and the best way to do this is by sending out consistent and valuable information.

You will need to employ a couple of components to give yourself the best chance of converting your leads into paying customers. To continue to nurture the prospect, we will need to add them to an email marketing campaign. There are a couple of techniques that you can go with when creating your email marketing campaign, but this is the most effective method that I have used so far.

1. Nurturing Email
2. Nurturing Email
3. Sales Email

I'm not sure where I first heard this saying, but every time I say it tends to raise a few eyebrows, but you must keep this same formula till they "buy or die." Let's begin this process from the beginning.

Ethical Bribe Delivery

Make sure this gets to them ASAP! Use automation tools to ensure that there is no lag time. The longer they wait, the harder it will be to turn them into a client. The subject of this email needs to be what they requested. Do not try and get fancy with this; there is simply no need. Keep it simple and just make the subject bar the headline of your Ethical Bribe: "Your Cheat Sheet

On The Six Ways To Live A Longer, Healthier Life!"

One thing that I have learned is that people do not like downloading items off of the internet. Ensure your Ethical Bribe is the content of the email and give them the option to download it with a PDF attachment if they wish.

After the Ethical Bribe is sent, how long do you wait to start the follow-up sequence?

Remember, you have successfully got them to take an interest in you. That is the hard part; now, all you have to do is nurture them and eventually turn them into a paying customer!

Follow Up #1

The first follow up is key to establishing a solid relationship. But when should you send it? The best time I have discovered to schedule a followup email is two days after they initially requested my Ethical Bribe. The time of day doesn't matter as much. Just average out when you have the best opening rate and apply that time for your sequence chain.

Now you know when to follow up, what should the email be about? Below is the basic outline of the strategy you need to use.

1. Talk about a problem your target market might have - Look at your Key Human Driver Statement and find a problem that boils down to their basic human desire if possible.
2. Explain how you solve the problem
3. Describe how life can look for the reader once the problem is solved - Make sure this is packed with benefits. Explain why they need it and how to get it.

The reason for the follow-up email is to solidify yourself as an expert in your field. The first follow up is just to continue to nurture and build this relationship. An example of a nurturing email that I would send would look something like this:

From: Cooper - WiseGuys

Subject: Should You Pay Someone To Maintain Your Facebook Page?

Dear (Name,)

Here at WiseGuys Digital Marketing, we are asked all of the time if it is necessary to pay someone to post on their Facebook page. While it can be a very simple way to build relationships and be seen by your target audience, we have seen a couple of problems with this in the past that you might want to consider.

Facebook posting isn't the most effective way to bring on clients for your company. So you must think if you are looking to get a return on investment, this is not the best avenue to do it. Another factor is that Facebook has made it more and more challenging to reach your followers by simply posting in recent years. Yes, you want to make sure it is active, but how much should you really be spending on this? We believe that if you took 10 minutes every two days and posted, that would be enough.

We even created an eBook with over 500 templates and examples that you could use to make sure that you never run out of ideas. Ensure that you are spending money on marketing avenues that will bring you a return on your investment.

Just click on the button down below, and I will send the eBook to you right away!

Sincerely,
Cooper

P.S. Our ebook will work for all of the other social media platforms as well. Ensure that you are focusing on one or two platforms that your target market spends the most time on, and post every two to three days!

(Posting on social media is a question that I get a lot from my clients, so I know that the leads I have generated wonder the same thing. Make sure you take down common questions that you get every day so you can use them for the followup emails.)

Follow Up #2

We're going to be sending another nurturing email. This one should be sent two days after the last email that you sent. Here's an example email of what I would send for my company, Bikes & Stuff.

Subject: Can You Bike When It Is Raining?

Dear (Name,)

Here at Bikes & Stuff, we are always asked if it is a good idea to bike in the rain. Sometimes you might just feel like riding in the rain, and other times you might get stuck in a storm that rolled in quickly. Simply put, yes, it is okay to ride in the rain, but you must follow a couple of tips that we have learned to ensure your safety.

Make sure you take corners slower than you usually would. When the concrete gets wet, your traction is significantly reduced. Also, make sure that you pack a pair of glasses to protect your eyes from the rain. If your bike does not have fenders make sure that you have them on, or you will shoot massive amounts of water on yourself. Buy lights and make sure cars can see you.

By making sure that you take all of the necessary precautions, you will stay safe and ride in the rain with ease!

Here's to living a long, healthy, and happy life!

Sincerely,
Coop

P.S. No matter how many precautions you take, you must ensure that you are always in control and wearing the proper safety equipment. We have a whole section of safety gear from lights down to helmets and protective gear. Stay safe, and have fun!

The key here is just giving them information to build the relationship. Think about these follow-ups as little dates. Just have a fun time, and simply get to know each other. You also are hitting on the KHD statement.

Follow Up #3

Depending on what industry you are in, you might want to give your target prospect a call rather than an email. Here is what the formula looks like for the Sales Follow-up if you are sending an email:

1. The problem they might have.
2. How you can solve that problem with your service.
3. Describe how amazing their life would look with emotion after you solve this problem.
4. A direct call to action directing them a sale.

Here's what an email would look like for WiseGuys:

Subject: Time To See Results From Your Marketing Efforts

Dear (Name,)

Are you tired of poorly performing marketing campaigns? Tired of all of the smoke and mirrors that come with marketing your company? When I bring on a new client, I am always amazed at the horror stories they tell me about their previous marketing experiences. When I explain our process and show them how we can generate their company consistent and dependable results, I can see them light up with enthusiasm.

Here at WiseGuys, we have developed a process that simply brings your business results. We walk through every step we will take and give you a complete overview to know what to expect.

Once you can consistently bring on the best clients, you will be overwhelmed with joyous emotions. How different would your business be if you were bringing on 10-20 new clients a week?

Right now, we are waiving all of our start-up fees for all of our packages. We want to ensure that we build trust and grow your business together.

To take advantage of this offer, give us a call at 816-318-7678 with promo code "email" or reply directly to this email, and we will give you a call!

Talk soon!

Cooper

P.S. We only have around seven spots left for this promotion. And no, I am not just saying this! We were finally able to get rid of our waiting list, and if you wait too long, you might be a part of it!

For your email marketing sequence, it should look like this:

1. Relationship building
2. Relationship building
3. Sales email and follow up

Repeat this email marketing sequence until they "buy or die." The key is to always be on their mind.

Remember, most of your prospects won't use your company until the eighth contact, so don't get down on yourself if they don't convert right away. Another critical aspect of email marketing is that you can keep in touch with your leads without paying "Big Tech."

Following Up With A Call

Now that you've sent at least three emails, you need to give them a quick call and introduce yourself. This is a major key to turning the lead into a paying customer. This isn't a cold call. It's actually the furthest thing from it. Take a step back and look at it from the potential client's viewpoint. They downloaded your Ethical Bribe and have read at least three of your follow up emails. You are practically their best friend at this point! Make sure you have confidence when you call and have fun with it! If you're tense, the lead will feel uneasy. Smile and have a good time.

Deciding Who To Call

How do you decide if you should call a prospect? Depending on the email marketing software you use, it will show you who has been opening up your emails consistently. If you're seeing that a group of leads is opening every single email, give them a call. This is one of the best leads you will ever get, and as long as you provide value with every interaction, you will have plenty of these leads to call on.

What To Say

Below is the basic outline of what you will say when you get a lead on the phone. Depending on your industry, you might want to switch up a couple of things, but the foundation will always stay the same. When you make the call, it will sound something like this:

"Hello, (Their Name!) My name is Cooper From XYZ Electric! I have been seeing that you have been opening up our emails, and I just wanted to call and personally introduce myself. Are you finding the emails are helping you with some of your household projects?"

This question will go either one of two ways. They will say yes, they are very helpful, or no, I am still having trouble. If they say yes, they are great; here is what to say.

"Awesome! Is there anything you would like me to write about?"

If they say your emails are not helping them with their household projects, you need to ask them if they want to schedule an appointment to come out and personally check it out for them.

No matter what they say, you're just trying to help them live a better life. For service-based businesses, it's vital to understand the long term objective. They might not need an electrician right now, but as soon as they do, who do you think they are going to call? I guarantee they are going to call your company every single time.

This might look like a lot of work in the beginning, but the return will be amazing. How often has a company not only added value to your life but called and asked you personally what they could do better?

Do you see how different this method is compared to what most companies do? Our clients at WiseGuys do not have to worry about bringing on new clients or making sales.

They always have plenty of clientele because they take time and truly cultivate relationships with their target market. They make it easy for their clients to refer them to their friends and family because they know you will treat them with respect and get the job done right.

It's not the easiest way to bring your company a "quick buck." It does take work, but at the end of the day, when it is all said and done, you will be happy you took the time to implement this strategy.

Cultivate Your Golden Egg

When you continuously grow this massive stockpile of your target clientele, it will be just like sitting on a gold mine. Before this stockpile turns into your own personal Golden Egg, you must make sure you are taking care of it and doing what is necessary for it to thrive. Once you do this, you will be able to profit off it for years to come!

Sales Team

After a few months of using this strategy, you will notice that you have far too many leads for just yourself to handle. Instead of neglecting your Golden Egg, I want to teach you the best way to hire a sales team without taking a massive risk.

The first key to hiring a salesperson is that they will be commission only, making a percentage of sales that they bring in. Let's say an average job brings in $2,400, and you have agreed to pay them a 20 percent commission for every sale they bring in. On average, they make six sales. The salesperson's average weekly income is $2,880. Times that by four, and they are making close to a six-figure income.

You can set it up however you want, but the key is to build out this sales team so that your business keeps growing. The important aspect that you must communicate with them is this: leads are the hard part of any sales job, right now; your company is bringing on 20-30 leads a week, and you simply cannot handle the load.

Break down the numbers right in front of them, and

show them the massive amount of earning potentially available to them. They would be stupid not to join your company.

Once you find someone for this position, you can let go of that responsibility and free up some time to improve your product or service. Continue to bring on more and more sales associates, and slowly build more and more team members until you are on track to achieving your Grand Strategy.

Ensure that no matter what industry you are in, hire killer sales members to bring in clients for your business. This will be key to the longevity of your business.

Implementing For Personal Services

For personal services like Financial Advisors, Accountants, Business Consultants, etc. Everything is going to stay the same until your follow up call.

If you're in the personal services industry, you will have a better chance of closing a prospect right then and there. If you work business-to-business, make sure you are talking to the decision-maker. When you notice that a prospect is consistently opening up your emails but not biting, my clients use the following process, which generates impressive results.

The first step you need to do is create an amazing offer and send it to them from your personal email. As soon as they open up the email, give them a call. Here's a loose script on what you should say.

"Hey, (prospect's name!) It's Cooper?" (It's important to start the conversation as if they are your best friend.) "Is this a good time?"

"I just personally wanted to reach out and introduce myself to you! How are you liking the email and the content I have been sending you?" Use an open-ended question to get them talking.

"I really thought the one I sent to you about (topic relating to their industry) was a good one for you."

"The reason for the call is to see if there was a time we could sit down and see if I could show you 'the main benefit they will get from your company? Are you free either Monday or Tuesday at 10 am?"

There are a couple of points that I want to hit on in this conversation. The first thing is that when you call, make sure that you do not sound like a telemarketer. You're greeting them by their first name as you would to your best friend.

If you call with the typical, "Hi, (Prospect Name,) my name is Cooper from WiseGuys. How are you doing today?" the rest of the conversation will be an uphill battle. When you greet them as a friend, their defenses will be down, and the conversation will start off great!

The second thing you must do is state your name as if they should and do know you. The best way to say your name is almost as a question, like Cooper? It is almost like saying you remember me, right?

The prospect will more likely than not reply with, "Oh yeah, of course! How are you?"

The third thing you need to do is ask open-ended questions. The more they talk, the better they will feel; you will also get valuable information that you can use later down the road to help close the sale.

The fourth thing you must do is point out a specific email or specific aspect of your Ethical Bribe that you feel really could have helped the prospect. This shows that you really care about them, and they will really appreciate this. It will also get them talking!

The fifth thing to do is ask for a meeting or appointment to show them how you can "the main benefit they receive from your company." Refer to your Key Human Driver Statement to ensure that you communicate the right message.

Depending on the business you are on, you could use the first, or the second strategy for calling. The first strategy is better for service-based businesses that people need every once and awhile. The second strategy is really for if you are in sales and can close the prospect on a specific product or service.

Tips To Help Your Overall Email Marketing Strategy

Email Marketing will be one of the most important tools for your company in your quest to convert leads into paying customers. I wanted to give you some additional tools to help you in the world of Email Marketing.

Tip #1: Every email that you send needs to provide some sort of value to your leads.

Tip #2: One of the main reasons someone opens an email is the sender's name. Make sure you use either your first name or your business name. For example, if your email is sent from "Sales Team," it will most likely not be opened.

Tip #3: Make sure all of your headlines pop. Bold claims or mystery work best when trying to get opens for your email marketing campaigns.

Tip #4: Make sure you are scheduling and creating your emails at least two weeks in advance. Make sure you are consistent with the time and frequency of your campaigns.

Tip #5: Always make sure you are taking the time to grow your email list. For most people, their email rules their lives. This is the best way you can keep in touch with your prospects.

Text Message Marketing

If you were able to grab their cell phone number, text message marketing is one of the best ways to get in touch with your lead. Your strategy must be a bit different here, though.

If you treat text message marketing like email marketing, you will really upset people quickly. Here are the guidelines that I've set for my clients to ensure that you don't piss off your lead.

You can use text message marketing to deliver your Ethical Bribe or anything that they have requested from you. You may also use it once a month to remind them of a special that you have at the moment. Please don't use it more than that, though. If you do, leads will drop off very quickly, and conversions will go way down.

Calling

Now, let's say that the industry you are in typically does not follow up with leads by calling. What should you do? Should you do what everybody else does? No! Call your leads, introduce yourself. It will be even that more special if they are not expecting it. They will remember this interaction for a long time.

For example, when my company started growing and hiring more people, I needed a way to make sure my processes were flawless. I was looking around and stumbled upon a Trainual advertisement on Facebook. I decided to give the application a try and see if I liked it.

After going through the tutorial and creating a couple of courses for my backend team, I wanted to take some time to see if there were any other options that I should try. So I logged out and continued on with the rest of my day. Two or three days after I signed up for the free tutorial, my phone rang, and to my surprise, it was the CEO of Trainual asking me how I was enjoying it and if there was anything he could do to make my experience better.

I told him that I loved the platform and that I am

going to get all of my training materials on there by the end of the month! It wasn't a massive gesture, but the fact that he took the time to call me and ask my option and what they could do better really made an impression on me.

To this day, I have never received any calls from any online platforms or services that I have signed up for other than Trainual. I won't even look at Trainual's competitors. Why? Because they took the time to really get to know me.

He wasn't calling me to sell me on the service. That wasn't the main point of the conversation. He was genuinely trying to get to know my company and me. He didn't say one word about upgrading or starting the paid subscription, but you know what I did as soon as we got off the phone? I went to his site and bought the paid subscription.

People love to buy but hate getting sold.

The best way to convert a lead into a client is to continuously build the relationship with value. You must take the time to understand people and what will influence them on a subconscious level. Be able to communicate what they are truly wanting to hear, rather than all of the normal puke they are used to getting.

Provide solid and consistent value that will help your prospect live a better life, give them tips and pointers about your industry that they might not know about. When you're giving them useful content every time they hear from you, they will choose your company when needed. Value isn't just in marketing pieces. Ensure that you give them a reason to continuously use your company by introducing new services and products to solve problems they have.

After the fourth email, pick up the phone and introduce yourself. You will be amazed by the amount of positive feedback you will receive from this small action. Let them know you care, and you are truly just wanting to see how you can make their lives better. Most of the time when I tell my clients that they will have to make sales calls, they imagine the Wolf of Wall Street, but we are actually doing the opposite. You're just getting in touch and building the relationship.

After all of this is completed correctly, that is when the money and success come into play. If any of these aspects from the formula are missing, you will be terribly disappointed and see terrible results.

In the next chapter, I'm going to go over the entire process with you. I will walk you through, step by step, on what you will need to do to get amazing results from this process. This next chapter should help you implement this strategy with the least amount of hiccups possible.

Most people are looking for the elevator instead of taking the stairs. They want the easy route. You're different. You're going to create something special.

Chapter Eight: Conversions

SECRETS RECAP:

Your follow up sequence needs to look like this:

1. Nurturing email #1
2. Nurturing email #2
3. Sales email
4. Call Prospects
5. Repeat until they "Buy or Die!"

CHAPTER NINE: BUILDING FROM THE GROUND UP

Now that we have explored every step in the Vending Machine Marketing Plan, I want to walk through the whole process one more time.

Every step of this process is vital to the success of growing your business. Think of it like baking a cake, skip one step, and the whole cake will be ruined. This chapter is going to be your cheat sheet to ensure all of the steps are implemented correctly.

Step #1: Grand Strategy

In chapter one, we looked at the qualities of some of the most successful people and organizations throughout humanity. We discovered that they all possessed the ability to establish an end goal and build a plan to get there. They ignored short term gratification to ensure they reach their long term Grand Strategy. Humans these days are addicted to short, insignificant wins that genuinely mean nothing in the long run.

This is good for us, though. We understand the importance of choosing our end goal and creating a plan to achieve it.

When you are marketing your company, you must know where you want to go. Choose an end goal that scares you a bit, and don't tell me the sky's the limit when humans have been to the moon. Let your competitors run in place, throwing marketing dollars out the window.

"In a world where people are increasingly incapable of thinking consequently, more animal than ever, the practice of Grand Strategy will instantly elevate you above the others."
– Robert Greene

If you are not sure where you want to go, your business will be like a ship without a rudder. Choose your end goal so we can build a plan to get there.

Step #2: Identify Target Market

I hope, by now, you understand the importance of being able to identify your target market. When you try to please everyone one, your company is like a simple bowl of carrots. Yes, if it were the last thing on earth, almost everyone would eat them. But they are not, and when you try and market a boring bowl of carrots, you will lose.

Who's your Target Market? Make sure you have a complete understanding of who they are and what they are looking for. You will become the industry leader, so you must understand the needs of the clients thoroughly. Jeff Bezos knew the problems of book readers. What problems does your target market have?

Instead of being everyone's last option, be a few's first option.

Step #3: Influencing Target Market

Now that we know who we are trying to target, we can build a plan to influence them. In this chapter, we took the time and looked at a few examples of how Cambridge Analytica was able to swing entire elections based on these principles. I used these examples to show how powerful these techniques are.

When trying to influence your target market, you must bypass the neocortex and speak directly to the brain's limbic part. Humans are highly emotional creatures, and if you want them to use your company, you must speak to their emotions. You must paint an image in their mind of the emotions they will feel if they do or don't buy your product. To do this, you must identify which one of the eight basic human desires your business helps solve.

Mercedes-Benz understands which human desires they must speak to if they want to sell cars. They know people do not buy expensive cars to get from point A to point B. If they did, Mercedes-Benz would be out of business. They sell a status symbol, to be superior, to keep up with the Joneses. All of their advertisements fall back on this simple principle, and it works like a charm.

Just like Mercedes-Benz, after you identify the basic desire that your business solves, you will use this as a starting point for all of the advertisements you create. Every ad that we create will have the underlying message of the basic human desire that will speak to humans' emotional side and drive action. What is your Key Human Driver Statement?

Step #4: Establish The Fundamentals

Just like the Wright brothers, we must get the basics down before ever running a marketing campaign. These are the fundamentals of your online presence, and without them, marketing will be a terrible experience.

Facebook

Your Facebook business profile needs to be aesthetically pleasing and filled in with all of the correct information. If your Facebook profile looks crummy, the potential client will most likely conclude that your business is also crummy.

Humans process visuals faster than words; that is why it is essential to make sure your Facebook profile is pleasing to the eye. Ensure your website, phone number, business address, and hours are correct and properly aligned with your Google My Business information.

When you are posting on Facebook, keep it light and fun. Encourage your audience to interact with your posts. The more interactions you get, the more people will see your post. Use Facebook to build solid relationships with your target market. Make them feel like they are a part of your business. Show them behind the scenes, ask them questions, get them involved. When potential customers are researching your company, make sure your Facebook builds trust with your potential customers instead of losing it!

Google My Business

The first step for Google My Business is to make sure that you create or claim your business profile. Once you get access to your GMB profile, make sure all of the information is correct. Remember, you want to make sure that your name, address, and phone number are all the same across the web. If not, Google will tax your ranking heavily. Add photos, and make sure it is aesthetically pleasing. Google My Business will be one of the main ways you will bring in new clientele if set up correctly.

Make sure that generating reviews for your company is the top priority on your to-do list. Without reviews, bringing on new clients will be an uphill battle. Make it easy for your happy customers to leave reviews by sending them an email or text with the link.

Website

When it comes to websites, everyone has their opinions. When a client asks me, "What makes a good website?" I typically reply with, "What do you want to get out of it?"

If you are like 99 percent of business owners in the world, your website is genuinely just a place where you can show off previous work and give your potential customers a place to learn more about your business. Your website needs to be kept very simple and should be easy to navigate. Make sure it is easy to view on mobile devices, and the load times need to be quick. Other than that, your website is whatever you want it to be.

Local SEO

Local SEO was created for businesses that operate in a particular geographic location. When you search for "Pizza in Kansas City" in Google, the Map Pack will be the first thing that pops up. If you are a business that wants to be at the top of this list, you need to make sure that your Google My Business is active and generate massive amounts of five-star reviews.

You need to make sure that your Name, Address, and Phone Number (NAP) are correct all across the internet on sites such as Yelp, Facebook, Google My Business, and all of the other local listing sites. Use tools like BrightLocal to identify and fix these problems.

Local SEO is a complete subject within itself, but doing these couple of things will drastically increase your business's rankings online.

Step #5: Your Bait

Now that you have the fundamentals in place, it is time to create the Ethical Bribe that your target market will want in exchange for their contact information. Trying to sell to potential customers on the first interaction is a formula for disaster. We need to build a relationship, and this is the first step in the process.

When you are creating the Ethical Bribe, make sure you are packing it with all of the amazing benefits of using your company.

Teaching why they need it, and then showing them how to get it. Establish yourself as an expert in your field, and show them that you are the obvious choice. When creating your Ethical Bribe, make sure it is communicating to your Key Human Driver Statement. Humans buy with emotions and justify with logic. Paint the picture in their minds of how amazing their lives with be when they buy your product or how miserable they will be if they decide not to buy your product.

Here is a vital part of the Ethical Bribe that you must make sure that you understand. People hate getting sold but love to buy. Don't come off as "salesy." Just inform them of your company's benefits.

Once you have created your Ethical Bribe, you need to create a headline that will catch your entire target market's attention, not just the 10 percent in the market to buy. For example, a good headline looks like this, *"The Top 5 Ways Homeowners Can Save Up To 50% On Their Electricity Bill This Winter!"* We also split test this version of the headline for parents with elementary school children. *"Looks like Santa Got A Budget Increase! The Top 5 Best Ways Homeowners Can Save Up To 50% On Their Electricity Bill This Winter!"*

I don't care who you are; everyone wants to save money on their electric bill. The HVAC company that we created this advertisement for was generating, on average,

15-20 leads every single day during their "slow season." All of the leads we generated were added to our nurturing process, and 22 percent ended up converting. So much for it being their "slow season."

Step #6: Create Advertisements

This step in the process should be the quickest and easiest step in this whole process. We have already done all of the backend work, not it is just time to plug and play. There are two main forms of online marketing: Social Media Marketing and Search Engine Marketing. I always choose avenues that allow me to gather leads from the actual platform rather than go to my landing page. If that's not an option, don't worry. We have already covered how to create a landing page that will convert traffic into leads.

In this chapter, I also discussed the importance of split testing your advertisements against each other. Make sure you create the bracket and testing the advertisements against each other. This will enable you to find the best advertisement to run for your company.

After you split test, and find the advertisement that you want to run, slowly increase the amount of money you put into the advertisement. The more money you make from the campaign, the more money you put into it. Keep repeating this cycle and continue to level up your business. Hire more sales members, hire more employees, and keep this cycle of growth going!

Step #7: Capture The Lead

There are two ways you will be able to capture a lead with your Ethical Bribe. The first and preferred method is to capture the lead directly from the platform. The reasoning behind this simple, you want to lead to be able to give you their information in the quickest way possible.

If they have to leave the platform they are currently on and go to a landing page; it will significantly decrease the amount of traffic that converts into a lead. They also feel safe on the platform they are on, and when they have to leave the platform and go to your landing page, it raises some defensive flags in the limbic parts of the brain.

The second method is to send them to your landing page. I know it seemed like I was insulting the landing page's entire existence, but they still are 100 times better than sending them to your main site. They also are amazing for platforms that don't allow you to capture leads. If you are unable to collect the leads directly from the platform, use landing pages!

Step #8: Conversions

Now that you have the lead, you need to slowly guide transform them into a paying customer. We've all seen the individual at the bar that is overly persistent when trying to get their desired spouse. It's awkward, and most of the time, outright creepy.

Now, look at the individual that has plenty of options when choosing their desired spouse. They are cool as a cucumber, not over the top persistent and annoying, and takes the time to truly get to know the person. They build a relationship before asking for the close.

Converting leads into paying customers works the same way. Build that relationship. We got their contact information, not we just need to keep sending them valuable information that will improve their lives and give them time to get to know us.

The follow-up sequence should look like this:

- Nurturing Email #1
- Nurturing Email #2
- Sales Email or Call
- Repeat Until They Buy

The more leads you have, the more conversions you will get. This massive stockpile of leads is your Golden Egg, and you need to make sure you properly nourish and cultivate it. Don't be afraid to call the leads that open your emails consistently and introduce yourself. In every single instance that I have done this, I have found myself having the time of my life. When you call just to connect with another individual with zero alternative motives, that is when you will truly grow your Golden Egg and build a massively loyal following.

Eventually, it will become self-sufficient, and your Golden Egg will grow all by itself, but it starts here. Take the time to set up an amazing nourishing process, and transform lives!

No, this process is not a get rich quick formula. Creating a business that dominates industries takes time, and as the old saying goes, "If it were easy, everyone would do it!" I personally like it when a project or task is difficult. Why? Because I know there is no traffic on the extra mile, it is lonely at the top for a reason. We are cut from a different cloth, and when you finally reach the peak of the mountain and completely dominate your industry, you will know it was all worth it.

PART 3
WRAPPING IT UP

For the last section of this book, I wanted to give you two additional pieces of information that you can use to continuously expand and grow your business. I'm going to share the best way to perform market research for your company. I will walk you through these methods step by step to help you find underserved customers in your target market. Once you're able to find them, you can capitalize on them.

The second chapter in this section is going to break down the basics of consumer psychology. I want to ensure that every aspect of your business is influencing your target market to buy from you instead of your competitors. I also give you a couple more examples of the best ways to implement them in your Vending Machine Marketing Plan.

These last two chapters help me add turbo boosters to the marketing plans I create, and I know it will help you tremendously as well!

CHAPTER TEN MARKET RESEARCH

This chapter will walk you through two of the best ways to conduct market research for your company using the tools digital marketing has to offer. The best part about both of these techniques is that the only thing you need is a free afternoon and a solid internet connection. If you're feeling stuck or simply want to understand your target market better, this is the chapter for you.

The One-Star Improvement Plan

The One-Star Improvement Plan will show you what your target market is most fed up with and give you a massive opportunity to fix it. Some of the world's biggest companies started by finding a problem in an industry and creating a solution to fix it.

You see, businesses are always trying to solve problems, and to do that, you must understand the problems your potential customers are having. Here's the trick though, most of the time, your potential customers have no idea what they want; all they know is that they are unhappy. When you send out surveys and spend massive amounts of money to ask them how their experience was, they either lie or don't respond. So how in the world can you improve or find a new corner of the market if even the potential clientele has no idea what they truly want? By comparing all of the unsatisfied reviews on Google.

The day I stumbled upon the One-Star Improvement Plan, I was sitting in my client's office, trying to think of ideas on how he can get ahead in his market.

As I pondered, I asked him, "What do electricians do that really pisses people off? What can we fix about the industry?" He sat there, looked at me for a minute, and then shrugged.

After a moment of silence, it hit me. Google might be the solution, thousands of reviews are written every day, and most of them are constructive criticism! I told him to open up Google and search for "electricians in Kansas City" and read all of his competitors' one-star reviews.

Here is the list of the most common complaints we found:

1. Late / Didn't show up on the proposed time.
2. Rude
3. Uniform was dirty / No Uniform.
4. Unmarked Vans / Crazy Drivers
5. Didn't finish the job correctly

Pro Tip: Make sure that the complaint comes up at least six or seven times. Any less than that, you might be wasting your time.

I knew we had stumbled across something special. After we had the list down, I asked a simple question, what could we do to solve these problems? Here are the solutions that we came up with:

On the company vans, we installed a tracking system so that the client can get an accurate estimate of when the electrician was going to show up. If the electrician were running behind, the GPS would alert the customer. We were able to get the time estimates within 15 minutes of the original estimated time. On top of that, the customer had to make an account to track when the electrician was going to show up, giving us their email address, which we used to generate massive amounts of positive reviews and add to his Golden Egg.

Rude electricians? This was an easy problem to fix. I asked my client if he feels that any of his guys might be short-tempered or rude to the clientele, and if so, get rid of them immediately. Your employees are the face of your business. If they go to a job and make the customer upset, that could result in millions of dollars in lost revenue over time.

Dirty, or no uniform? Another easy fix. Before the electrician went out on the job, they were inspected. Clean shave, clean haircut. Clothes fit properly and a matching uniform with a name badge on their shirt. There is nothing more confusing than someone coming to your home to do work, and they look like they just rolled out of bed. Do you honestly believe that the client will refer you to their friends and family? "Oh yeah! I had an electrician come to my house today. He was rude, smelled like a barn, and looked like he just rolled out of bed! Want his number?" Make sure your employees are looking for the part.

Wrapping your work vans is a must in today's day and age. Invest the amount and make sure your van looks professional! You also will get your name out there when you are driving around town. When you are at someone's home, you want the neighbors to see your company. With the example earlier in this book, if you want to dominate a specific market in a neighborhood, this is critical! When it comes to crazy driving, that goes along with making sure the employees are right. You also can install speed trackers and dash cams.

Again, easy fix. Before the electrician leaves the property, make sure that they show the client what changes they made and make sure they are happy. Another thing you make sure they do is to ask them if there are any other problems they are having around the house. This will give your electrician a chance for a potential upsell.

In this scenario, my client had been working with me for quite some time, and his Vending Machine Marketing Plan had cultivated his business a massive Golden Egg. We created a sales email and described all of the massive changes we had made, and how we were dedicated to always improving his customers' experience.

The day the email was sent, my client set up so many appointments that he was booked out for a solid month. We even had to hire a couple more electricians. That being said, his company is growing at an exponential rate compared to his competitors. All of this for one afternoon of research, incredible.

You see, it isn't necessarily that these changes were that drastic or game-changing. What really meant a lot to his target market and potential clients is that he took the time and really understood their needs and created a plan to solve them.

We also created an Ethical Bribe detailing all of the drastic changes we made. This only added fuel to the fire, and his Golden Egg will refer him to their friends and family for many years to come.

The One-Star Marketing Plan Checklist:

- Select The Industry
- Read All Of The Poor Reviews
- Find The Most Common (Max 3-4)
- Develop A Solution
- Inform Your Golden Egg
- Market Your Solution • Repeat
- Dominate Your Pond

The second method you can use to gather market research for your company is a technique that I call Dominate Your Pond. What we are going to do is use all of the tools of online marketing to find underserved customers in your marketplace.

This is a method I have been using in one form or another for a very long time and has completely changed the way I approach marketing for not only my clients but also for all my companies. I never had a clear, defined process until I ran across Glenn Livingston, PH.D. He calls his process "The Bull's-Eye Social Media Technique," and as I was reading the article, I saw the massive similarities between my process and his. Below is a combination of his method and mine, enjoy!

The first step to dominating your pond is choosing ONE keyword phrase that describes your business online. You must make sure your target market is defined, so this should be no problem for you. Don't worry about "excluding your potential customers" because we know, "Rather than being everyone's last choice, be a few's first option."

Once you have your one keyword phrase, you need to make sure that it has enough traffic to be worth pursuing. Google has a keyword tool that will show you how many searches a month, this keyword phrase has, and if your competitors are paying to be found for this keyword. For example, if I owned a bike shop, this is what my keyword search would look like.

Now that we know that there are customers searching for mountain bikes, and my competition is paying to be found under this keyword, we can move onto the next step. (For mountain bikes, it is almost a given that there are many searches and very high competition. This is really for the people with the keyword phrases that are very specific, like "underwater pottery classes for children."

Once you have your one keyword phrase, the first thing that you must do is put quotes around your phrase and paste it into search.twitter.com. What I am looking for is tweets or conversations that show any type of frustration in the market or any wishes the prospect of customers might have.

Go to all of the social platforms like Facebook and YouTube and try and find the most information you can on this specific industry. Make sure you are taking notes on the things that are coming up repeatedly on either a Google Doc or a sheet of paper. Don't try and memorize this list. Facebook groups can be a massive key to understanding the true problems of a specific marketplace. This is my secret key to getting to know the industry and the problems they are truly having. If I were trying to gather information for my bike shop, I would hop on Facebook and look for a "Mountain Bike Group" and read the posts within that group. If you can join the group, do so. Get involved and post questions about what they wish the market offered and what they are really looking for. If you find the right group, you can gather information that will completely change your business forever.

To find your Facebook Group, head over to Facebook and type in your industry in the search bar, and click the option for "Groups" and it will pull up all of the groups for that keyword. This will be your true money pit. Read the posts and try and add some value here and there. Do not post anything about your business; for now, be another member of the group.

The next step to gather information is to search blogs for your keyword. To do this, go to https://blog.google and read the top blogs for your industry. Again, you are looking for a common frustration that more than a handful of people are experiencing.

Once you have gathered all of the relevant information from the tools above, you need to focus on the most passionate and engaging problems. Is there a common problem that keeps coming up that you can solve? Is there anything missing from the market? The key here is finding a common problem that your target market is frustrated with.

You are looking for one thing that will separate you from your competitors and help you stand out for your one keyword phase. What is the one key difference that can separate you from your competitors?

Once you feel like you have a complete understanding of your target market's frustration, now it is time to confirm that this is a real problem, that the target market actually needs a solution for.

Now that you have gathered all the information and have found what is truly lacking in your target market, you will need to go back to the Facebook groups you joined and ask them if this solution would drastically improve their lives. Ask at least 30 people, and if they all say yes, you can run with the idea. If not, they will point you in the right direction.

Another key benefit of this exercise is that you will get a completely different view of the marketplace and what their needs truly are. Once you find the one key difference between your competitors and yourself, you will be able to completely dominate your pond. Dominate Your Pond Checklist

- Define Your Single Keyword Phrase
- Search Social Media Sites
- Join A Facebook Group
- Discover Key Problem
- Ask Target Market If They Like Your Idea
- Run With It

The reality for most businesses trying to find ways to improve is like trying to make a freethrow with your eyes closed, but it doesn't have to be that way. These methods are designed to help you get a complete understanding of what your target market wants without paying a small fortune to a market research company.

Take the two methods I have given you, find a problem(s) that your target market is having, infuse it into your Vending Machine Marketing Plan, and continue to grow your company. Cultivate your Golden Egg, and be the key player in your industry.

CHAPTER ELEVEN: BREAKING DOWN PSYCHOLOGY

Understanding the way humans think and behave is a key aspect of marketing your company effectively. Without this knowledge, this journey would be like trying to drive from New York City to Los Angeles without a GPS or road map.

I am going to share all of the information that will help assist you in reaching your goals. Almost all of this information I have learned from the wonderful book called *How Psychology Works*. I highly recommend you buy it if you want to learn all about the way your mind works.

The Main Components That Drive Consumer Behavior

Consumer psychology is understanding how your customers behave—what they buy, what they need, and the factors that influence their buying habits and choices.

So, what drives consumer behavior? In the book, *How Psychology Works, they give six main reasons why people buy:*

Personal Recommendations - People like to buy the products that their friends and role models are using.

Reviews - Consumers read customer reviews to help them decide what to buy.

Brand Information - Consumers want to know what is in it for them if they buy a product.

Past Experience - People are driven by positive past experiences, so familiarity with a brand goes a long way.

Trust - Buyers need to be confident that a company will deliver on its promises and keep their data and bank details safe.

Promotions - Customers are attracted by promotions. Especially if they perceive greater value for money.

Pricing - Consumers buy when prices are at an affordable level that gives value for money. Careful pricing ultimately increases sales.

Now that we understand the main factors that influence consumers to buy, we must step back and make sure each of these factors is correctly implemented into your overall marketing plan.

Personal Recommendations

Being able to generate personal recommendations and referrals is the ultimate goal for any business. Without them, it will feel like rowing upstream against a raging current. This step isn't necessarily part of your marketing plan; it's the end goal. Our marketing plan is the spark for growing your Golden Egg. At a certain point, your business will reach a level where it will naturally grow all by itself.

Think about this whole process, almost like how a parent raises their child. At first, the newborn needs constant care and attention and can go for a very short time without their parents' help. The older they get, the more self-sufficient they become. Then one day, these children can do everything on their own. (for the most part)

Take care of your Golden Egg so that one day, it can grow and eventually become self-sufficient all by itself. Build loyalty and trust with your target market and generate massive amounts of personal recommendations and referrals. For this to happen, though, we must make sure the following steps are followed and correctly implemented.

Reviews

Chapter four discussed your Google My Business profile and the importance of generating reviews from previous clientele. This must be one of your top priorities if you want to grow your Golden Egg.

With this being one of your fundamental building blocks to grow your business, you must make sure you are doing everything in your power to gain as many reviews as possible. With companies like Amazon, we have become such a review-based society that the only key factor we look at is the number of five-star reviews they have.

For example, let's say you are in the market for a new roof; you ask a few buddies and see if they have one they would recommend. Your friend Brad tells you that XYZ Roofing is the best in town, and you should definitely use them. You thank him for his time and decide to do a bit more research before making the call.

If you are anything like me, you're going to Google the company and look at their reviews. More and more people are taking the side of the reviewers than personal recommendations from friends and family.

To your amazement, XYZ Roofing has 20 reviews, and over half of them are of upset customers. XYZ Roofing is rated overall, 2.1 out of 5 stars. You begin to wonder why in the world your friend "Brad" decided to recommend this company. Did he somehow know the owner? Dating the owner's daughter? You choose to keep searching and not use the XYZ Roofing company after all.

Let's step back and look at it from Brad's vantage point; he might have had an amazing experience with the XYZ Roofing company. After informing him I decided to go with another company, instead of his recommendation, he hops on Google and searches for the XYZ Roofing Company. To his amazement, he sees the awful ratings that XYZ has accumulated. Embarrassed, he calls me, offering an apology. You see, he would have never even recommended the XYZ Roofing Company if he knew how bad their ratings were online, even though his experience was phenomenal.

There is a double-edged sword to making sure your business has an amazing online reputation. The first reason is that if you have a poor rating online, no one in their right mind will use your company, and Google will not let you be found on organic searches. The second reason is that even if someone like Brad has an amazing experience with your brand, he will not refer you to his friends and family once he sees your online rating. This is going to hinder your Golden Egg's growth. If it's not taken care of, it'll eventually kill it.

If you have workers in the field, create an incentive to get reviews, say a $25 bonus for every review they get from happy customers. Make sure you are making it very easy to leave your company a review. In chapter four, I showed you how to create the link to send to your happy customers.

Have you done some work for your sister? Ask for a review. It doesn't matter if they are friends or family; if you have done any work for them, you need to make sure they leave your company a review.

Take the time and generate as many reviews as possible for your business. My recommendation for my clients is to get at least ten five star reviews a month. After just two years, your company would have accumulated over 240 five-star reviews, and the more you have, the bigger your Golden Egg will become.

Brand Information

When someone is deciding which company to use, they want to understand what the experience will be like before they use your company. How much information do you have on the world wide web about your company?

Let's imagine you are trying to find a plumber in your area. You ask your friends, and Sarah recommends ABC Plumbing. You hop on Google and search for the company like you always do.

After you hit search, there is nothing about the ABC Plumbing company, and you start to wonder if Sarah got the name right. None of the profiles are set up, and the only thing they have is an outdated website. How were you even supposed to judge this company without any information? You decide to keep asking around.

When a potential customer searches for your brand online, you need to make sure you have a strong presence for your company. Your Google My Business profile needs to come up with massive amounts of positive reviews, your online profiles need to be created or claimed, and your website needs to be filled with educational blogs and videos. You also need to make sure you included pictures of your previous work and client testimonial videos, if possible.

Again, they're trying to get a feel for what it will be like to use your company. You need to show off your previous work and let them know right away that you are an expert. Your potential clients want to see that new faucet you just installed.

Remember back in high school when your math

teacher made you show "proof of work" or you didn't get credit? This is your proof of work to your potential clientele. You may think that a simple faucet installation is boring, and no one wants to see a simple picture of this, but they do.

When you take the time and post a blog once a week on your site, or upload videos of clients, it is painting a picture in their mind of how it will be to work with your company. This is your proof of work. Show your potential clientele that you can, and you will take care of them because you have done it before. The more you can put online, the better. Simple as that.

Past Experience

You may be asking yourself right now, "If we are trying to bring on new clientele that has never used our company before, how in the world can we take advantage of past experience? Are we simply out of luck?" You're not out of luck, and here's why.

Remember our Ethical Bribe and all of the nurturing we are doing? This is going to help with the past experience part of the decision making process. When you deliver value to them and continue to follow up and nurture them, they will develop trust and familiarity with you.

Past experiences do not necessarily mean that they have bought your products or services; it means that the interactions that they have had with your company have been positive thus far.

That's another reason why creating Ethical Bribes and

nurturing the relationship is so important. Before they even use your company, they already associate you with Value and familiarity.

The more time you take in creating your Ethical Bribe and create a flawless nurturing process, the more likely it will be that your target market will associate your business with positive experiences.

Trust

Does your potential customer trust that you will be able to deliver on your promises? Do they believe that you are capable of the task at hand? All of the steps in The Vending Machine Marketing Plan have been to win your target market's trust.

Creating Ethical Bribes, ensuring your online profiles are all in place, nurturing and educating, showing proof of work, and having an amazing online reputation are all keys to building trust between your company at the target market.

It seems that every day you hear about a company taking advantage of their clientele in one form or another. Entire industries are tainted by the terrible actions of one company or individual.

Right now, think of someone that you trust. What qualities do they possess that enabled you to trust them? Did you trust them right away? Most likely not. They had to show you that they are worthy of your trust. Depending on how quickly you develop trust for someone, it may take weeks, months, or even years to win their complete trust. One thing is for sure; actions speak louder than words.

When you are growing your Golden Egg, you must approach building trust in the same way you build it with another person. Rather than saying your company is the best, show it. Show your proof of work, show all of your happy clients, show that you are the expert, show that you are a company that can be trusted.

Follow up with consistent and helpful information. Once you do this, clients will come flocking to your business. Remember, trust doesn't form with someone after one interaction, but if you make a wrong move, or screw your target market, all of that trust you built can vanish at the drop of a hat. Stick to your word, and establish your business as not only an industry leader but one that can be trusted.

Make sure that you are doing everything in your power to win the trust of your target market. If you don't, it will be almost impossible to cultivate and grow your Golden Egg.

Promotions

The best time to use promotions in the Vending Machine Marketing Plan is when you are sending your "Sales Follow-Up Email" with a specific deadline for the promotion. When promotions become a problem is when companies run so many that the customer waits until your next deal to use your company.

When you set up the VMMP correctly, you won't need

to run promotions to get customers to use your business. *Instead, you will attract customers who are happy to pay more, knowing that they are dealing with a true expert. Rather than just getting the customers that shop solely on price, you will get serious buyers who only want to work with the best.*

To me, promotions show desperation and should be used very sparingly at the beginning of cultivating your Golden Egg. Once you are bringing on a steady flow of clientele, the promotions should be slowly phased out and eventually abandoned completely.

If the only time your target market wants to use your company is when you are running a sale, you are in big trouble. Promotions should only be used to start the cultivation of your Golden Egg; once started, get rid of them!

Pricing

I get that you have to keep your prices competitive, and most companies say "competitive pricing" in their marketing pieces for some reason I have yet to comprehend fully. But it would be best if you remembered that pricing is all relative, and when you can show your target market that you are worth the extra money, they will pay for it.

Are you a Ritz-Carlton or a Holiday Inn? Same industry, way different price per night. The Holiday Inn will provide you with a room with a bed to sleep in just as the Ritz-Carlton will, but the Ritz-Carlton can charge five times the amount per night compared to the Holiday Inn.

While on vacation with my family, I booked us to stay

at the Ritz-Carlton in Beaver Creek, Colorado. As soon as we entered the hotel door, the staff immediately greeted us with big smiles and a polite, "How are you doing this evening, sir?" While checking in, the lady at the desk was very attentive and made us feel like welcomed guests.

Once we got to our room, there was a fire already burning, and on our main table, there was a note that read, "Think you are a WiseGuy, Eh?" with my favorite snack right next to it, a bowl full of Honey-Crisp Apples. My whole family looked at each other with amazement and let out a big laugh.

After we got settled, I grabbed the note and went down to the front desk and asked how in the world they knew that the name of my company was WiseGuys Digital Marketing?

The lady at the front desk explained that I had reserved the room under a company card, and the name on the card had my business name on it.

That made perfect sense, but how did they know that "Think you're a WiseGuy, Eh?" was my catch-phrase? And that I loved Honey-Crisp Apples? She told me that after I checked in, she searched my business on Facebook, and found my catch-phrase and saw that I posted about my love for Honey-Crisp Apples. Wow! Not only that, but they took the time to write out the note and get apples ready so that when I arrived, it would be a special moment for my whole family and me.

The next day, as we were heading out to ski on the mountain, our skis were already set up and ready for us to ride. You see, every single experience we had was first class, and from now on, no matter where I go in the world, if there is a Ritz available, I am staying there.

Price is relative to the value you are giving to your prospect. If price were the only thing that mattered, places like the Ritz-Carlton wouldn't exist. If your target market is giving you pushback on your prices, instead of lowering your prices, give more value!

Show them that you are worth the extra money and give more value before deciding to use your company! If someone tells you that your prices are too high, ask them, "What would I need to do to convince you that my company is worth this price?" This will prompt them to explain what they need to see to justify paying this amount. Once you can show them what they asked to see, they will be happy to pay the amount you charge.

People willingly pay five to ten times as much to stay at the Ritz than the Holiday Inn. They're both hotels at the end of the day, but the Ritz provides more value. The price is justified in the experiences that you get and the people you meet.

Instead of focusing on the price, figure out how you can add more value to your business so you will be able to charge more for your services. The first step in doing this is establishing yourself as an industry leader, an expert. You have already done this; now, all you must do is be willing to ask the price and demand to get it.

Changing Consumer Behavior

"A company's success depends on how well it sells its products to consumers, and that requires persuasion. At the heart of effective persuasion is the ability to change people's attitude" - How Psychology Works.

To persuade your target market to use your company, you need to influence their attitudes in a way that favors your company over your competitor. In *How Psychology Works*, they say that there are six principles of persuasive marketing that retailers and other businesses make full use of. Even if people resist persuasion initially, their attitude and behavior may be open to change over time.

They are:

1. *Commitment* - People feel like they are part of a community when companies give them a say in the product or service, such as issuing a membership card that offers discounts - and are more likely to buy.
2. *Authority* - Customers want to believe in leaders and salespeople. They look for credentials and experience and prefer to buy from someone who evidently knows their product and can sell them the most suitable type.
3. *Liking* - People are more inclined to buy from those who like, complement, or appreciate them. Expressing approval ("That Dress Looks

Great On You!") encourages a potential buyer to spend money with that company.
4. *Consensus* - Many people copy others, so they are more likely to change their behavior if others have done so. Here, a longer queue for one of two competing products is seen to suggest which is a better buy.
5. *Scarcity* - Products that seem rare are attractive, so companies find ways to make a product feel like a special commodity, for example, by displaying something on its own shelf that is hard to reach.
6. *Reciprocity* - It comes naturally to return kind gestures or reciprocate gift giving. If a company offers something, such as a free cookie, to prospective customers, they are more likely to feel compelled to buy there.

Looking back at our Vending Machine Marketing Plan, we can identify some of the methods that we have already set in place. I want to walk you through different examples of how you can use each one of these methods to grow your business.

Commitment

What are some ways you will establish a strong commitment between your business and your clientele? The best way is to make them feel like they are part of a tribe or family. Giving them special perks that "normal" people are not allowed to access. Things like special perk cards, insider lists, and membership perks are all ways to get your target market to truly commit to your business.

For example, if you are a "Nike Member," you get early access to new products a week or so before the rest of the marketplace. This makes you feel like you are a part of the company, an insider, and that they actually value their loyal customers.

What can you give to your customers that will help them commit to your business?

Authority

Establishing yourself as the authority is a massive part of your Vending Machine Marketing Plan. Ethical Bribes and creatine educational pieces regularly will cement your business as the authority in your industry.

Your customers want to know that you can understand their needs and find the best product for them. People will go out of their way and even pay more to deal with a true expert. Creating an educational video, writing blogs, and posting on social media will help you establish yourself as your industry's authority.

Taking time to block even one day out of the month to create educational pieces will do wonders for your company in the long run.

Liking

Simply put, people want to do business with people they like, complement, or appreciate them. The best way to implement this strategy in your marketing campaign is to say things like, "Oh, you want to learn how to grow your business? You are the type of person I want to be around!"

Complementing them on their interests is the only way you will be able to use this method effectively. If you are unable to see the person, there is no way you will be able to compliment them on their shoes or shirt. You can use this method when potential clients call your office or finally meet in person.

Consensus

When people wait for a product or service, it implies that whatever they are waiting for must be truly great. I mean, why else would they wait? Companies use this method to increase their brand's attractiveness, even though what they are selling isn't that different from their competitors.

People copy other people. Showing that other people are interested in your product or services will build on this trait and influence your target market to want to use your company.

Scarcity

Scarcity is a method that has been used by businesses to increase the worth of their products and services since the beginning of time. Commodities like gold, silver, and Bitcoin are all built on the principle of scarcity. There is only a certain amount globally, so they are valuable, even though Bitcoin is the only commodity with an actual finite amount of supply.

Some of the most famous examples of this are Kanye West's Yeezy shoe line. When Adidas Yeezy Boost 350 V2 first got released, they were sold out in as little as ten minutes. Why? Scarcity. Do you really believe that a brand like Adidas could have more if they wanted to? Of course, they could have, but that would have ruined the scarcity and, ultimately, the brand's value.

What can you do to increase the amount of scarcity in your business? Only offer certain amounts of products? Only sell a product during a certain time of the year? Scarcity is an amazing tool to increase sales for your company, but make sure you are not too "salesy" about it!

Reciprocity

It is basic human nature to want to return kind gestures or reciprocate when someone gives you something of value. In our nourishing process, we are actively using this part of basic human nature to eventually win over the business of our target clientele.

I have officially stopped going to the grocery stores on Saturdays for this reason alone; I am simply a sucker for reciprocity. Whenever I get a free sample, I always end up buying what the sampler is handing out that day. What can I say? I am a sucker for this form of persuasion, and I am sure your target market is too.

When creating your Ethical Bribes and the nurturing emails, make sure you are giving them massive amounts of value. The more value they feel like they received, the more likely they will want to reciprocate.

Before You Begin

There is one critical piece that you must possess before you can start to persuade your target market, and that is credibility. In my experience, the best way to generate credibility is to provide value and educate your target market. Go back to the basics. Without credibility, all of your attempts to persuade your target market will go unnoticed.

Consumer Neuroscience

What are the different aspects that affect the way we make decisions on which brand to use? Luckily for us, there are people that study this type of thing, and they are called neuroscientists. They specialize in studying the brain and the impact it has on a person's thought process and behavior.

Referring back to *How Psychology Works,* they state that "Rather than relying on what consumers tell them—and many individuals either cannot or chose not to express their preferences—neuro marketers see how the brain activity of volunteers is stimulated by emotions, the key to deciding whether to buy something."

"Research has shown, for instance, that activity increases in the *mesolimbic* (reward-linked) brain area when participants are shown cars they find attractive, and that people's decisions change when they are more hungry, stressed, or more tired than usual."

That being said, visual responses are the best way we'll be able to have a deep neurological impact. Having high-quality visuals draws customer attention and increases their engagement.

Now that you understand how important visuals are to your company's overall marketing and branding, let's look at the specific examples in *How Psychology Works.*

Infographics - Condensing data or information into a chart or diagram helps it lodge in the consumer's mind. It is said that a good infographic is worth a thousand words.

Fonts - How appealing the letters look and how easy they are to read affect whether the consumer wants to read the message they contain.

Videos - Moving images can tell a story well and appeal to consumers who are used to getting their information from television and video clips on the Internet or social media.

Memes - Wittily captioned photos, often ridiculing human behavior, are spread rapidly via social media. The combination of image and humor lodges an idea of a cultural symbol in the brain.

Symmetry and proportion - Symmetrical, wellproportioned images convey a sense of harmony, while asymmetry and distortion suggest dynamism or discord.

The Psychology of Color - Colors, above all, communicate mood and emotion and provoke a reaction. Designers and marketers choose color to fuse the nonverbal mood with the message the company or brand wants to get across.

- **Green:** Foliage and bright greens look restful and suggest a product is natural, healthy, restorative, reassuring, a new beginning, environmentally aware, and fresh. Darker, emerald green speaks to wealth.
- **Red:** Bright red gets a fiery response: exciting, sexy, passionate, urgent, dramatic, dynamic, stimulating, adventurous, and motivating. In a dangerous context, it can give an aggressive, violent, or bloody impression.
- **Blue:** Sky blue seems cool, dependable, serene, and suggestive of infinity, whereas bright blue crackles with energy. Dark blue has authority and is associated with professionals, uniforms, banks, and tradition.
- **Pink:** While light pink comes across as innocent, delicate, romantic, and sweet - sometimes verging on the sentimental - bright pink, like red, is a hot, sensual, attention seeking, energetic, and celebratory color.
- **Purple:** Linked to intuition and imagination, purple is a contemplative, spiritual, and enigmatic color, especially on the bluer side. Red-purples imply something more thrilling- creative, witty, and exciting.

Shapes - Geometric shapes make a product look dependable and familiar, whereas organic forms suit a creative idea. Straight edges and corners see more severe than curves and flowing lines.

Everything you do in terms of design for your company needs to be taken into massive consideration before it is introduced to your target market. You need to make sure that you can catch and hold your target market's attention with the fonts and colors you use.

Your website, logo, and marketing pieces all need to match and communicate the correct message to your target market.

The Power Of Branding

What do you want your customers to associate with when they buy your product or use your service? Developing your brand will distinguish your company from the rest of your competition. This creates a bond between the supplier and the customer. In *How Psychology Works,* they give five key characteristics that you can choose from when identifying your brand image.

They are:

- *Excitement* - Daring, cool, spirited, imaginative, up-to-date, independent, youthful.
- *Sincerity* - Down-to-earth, honest, familyoriented, wholesome, cheerful.
- *Ruggedness* - Tough, strong, outdoorsy, masculine.

- *Competence* - Reliable, hardworking, intelligent, corporate, successful, confident.
- *Sophistication* - Glamorous, good-looking, charming, smooth, feminine.

Being able to let people identify themselves with your brand is the quickest way to build a massively loyal following. Consumers identify themselves with the possessions they buy and see their possessions as a part of themselves. Most people's buying behavior is motivated by self-expression.

Iconic brands allow consumers to live out their desires about their identity. Companies like Harley-Davison have perfectly aligned themselves with who their consumers are trying to be. When you drive a Harley-Davidson, you're associating yourself with the brand identity of ruggedness.

Consumers can be who they want just by changing what they buy, projecting their chosen self-image via the brands they select or identify with. Make a choice right now. What brand personality are you wanting to identify with?

When someone uses your company, what does that mean for their personality? Clearly communicate the message to them. Make sure you take the time and identify your brand identity.

SECRETS RECAP:

Understanding the basics of consumer psychology is one of the fundamental building blocks to market your company successfully. Take the time to build your review, build brand information with proof of work, cultivate trust, selectively use promotions, and charge whatever you want.

Ensure you understand the different components of changing consumer behavior and create visuals that will grab your target market's attention. Let your customers associate themselves with your brand profile and dominate your competition!

CONCLUSION

Our journey together is now coming to an end. But before we part ways, I want to let you know it is perfectly normal to feel a bit overwhelmed by all of the steps and strategies in this book. I am the type of person that overthinks everything. I overanalyze and make tasks ten times harder than they need to be. My motto when I get overwhelmed is K.I.S.S. Keep It Simple, Silly. Take things one step at a time. If you start to get frustrated, remember K.I.S.S., and take a deep breath and relax.

Ultra-Wealthy companies understand that to make tons of money, you must influence people who have the money. Humans will be buying from your company, and you must understand them inside and out. You must speak to their emotions and communicate the correct message to give your businesses the best chance to transform them into paying clients.

After they take the time to choose their target market and develop a plan to influence them, they understand how to generate clients on a massive scale. They generate something of value in return for the individual's contact information. For companies like Amazon, it was a free trial of Amazon Prime. Ethical Bribes are the best route to go for companies that do not have a service that people can try out for 30-days.

Every interaction they have with the lead from then on is about cultivating the relationship and drawing on the emotional triggers that drive action. They know that the more you see them, the more likely the lead will convert into a paying client.

The wealthiest businesses treat their target market exactly how you build relationships with people in the real world. Humans love to buy but hate getting sold. When you create advertisements and try and sell someone based on one interaction, it is just like asking someone to get married right after meeting them. It simply doesn't make sense, and your conversion rates will be pitiful.

This method will transform you from just another business begging for new clientele, desperate and lonely, to a welcomed guest into your target market's life. You will feel like an old friend to your target prospects, and once you reach this point, you have won.

The best marketing in the world is all about understanding how to influence your target market and build a lasting relationship with them. Forget all of the short term B.S. If you want to create a massively successful business, this is the routine you need to take. If I could pin one word to describe the entire book, it would be relationships.

Now that you have a complete understanding of the Marketing Secrets of the Ultra-Wealthy, it is time to start implementing each step, one at a time. Below I have included the worksheet I use when working with my clients, and I want you to have it.

Follow along one step at a time, and if you have any questions, give me a call at 816-318-7678 or email me at cooper@wiseguysdigitalmarketing. com.

Conclusion

VENDING MACHINE MARKETING PLAN
WORKSHEET

Grand Strategy

_____
_____
_____
_____
_____

Target Market Profile

_____
_____
_____
_____
_____

Key Human Driver Statement

_____
_____
_____
_____
_____

Basic Fundamentals Created?

- Facebook
- Google My Business
- Website
- Education

Ethical Bribe & Headline

_____
_____
_____
_____
_____

Platforms Used For Ads

_____
_____
_____
_____
_____

Landing Page Created?

- Yes
- No

Conclusion

Email Marketing Topics For Nurturing

_____
_____
_____
_____
_____
_____
_____

KEY: Nurturing, Nurturing, Sales

Market Research Discoveries

_____
_____
_____
_____

New Methods Learned From Consumer Psychology?

_____
_____
_____
_____

Conclusion

Repeat & Improve

_____
_____
_____
_____

Thank you so much for reading. I pray that all of your wildest dreams are accomplished, and you live the life you truly deserve.

With massive amounts of love,

Cooper Saunders

Conclusion

Conclusion

Conclusion

Conclusion

Conclusion

Conclusion

Conclusion

Conclusion

Conclusion

Conclusion

Conclusion

Conclusion

Conclusion

Conclusion

Conclusion

Conclusion

Conclusion

Conclusion

Conclusion

Conclusion

Conclusion

Conclusion

Conclusion

Conclusion

Conclusion

Conclusion

Conclusion

Conclusion

Conclusion

Conclusion

ABOUT THE AUTHOR

Cooper Saunders is the owner and founder of WiseGuys Digital Marketing, located in Kansas City, Missouri. He has worked with companies across the United States to grow their revenue and increase their brand visibility. Simply put, he knows how to grow businesses with tried and true marketing methods, developed by analyzing some of the world's most successful companies.

www.ingramcontent.com/pod-product-compliance
Lightning Source LLC
Chambersburg PA
CBHW020638220526
45464CB00001B/196